JOSEPH A. FITZMYER, S.J.

# ACCORDING TO PAUL

## Studies in the Theology
## of the Apostle

Paulist Press
New York / Mahwah, NJ

Imprimi Potest
Rev. Edward Glynn, S.J.
*Praepositus Provinciae Marylandiae*

Nihil Obstat
Rev. Richard J. Murphy, O.M.I.
*Censor Deputatus*

Imprimatur
Rev. Monsignor William J. Kane
*Vicar General for the Archdiocese of Washington*
13 July 1992

The *nihil obstat* and *imprimatur* are official declarations that a book or pamphlet is free of doctrinal or moral error. No implication is contained therein that those who have granted the *nihil obstat* and *imprimatur* agree with the content, opinions, or statements expressed.

*Library of Congress Cataloging-in-Publication Data*

Fitzmyer, Joseph A.
    According to Paul : studies in the theology of the Apostle /
Joseph A. Fitzmyer, S.J.
    p.    cm.
    Includes bibliographical references and indexes.
    ISBN 0-8091-3390-3
    1. Paul, the Apostle, Saint.   2. Bible. N.T. Epistles of Paul —
Theology.   I. Title.
BS2651.F49   1992
225.9′2 — dc20                                   93-20453
                                                   CIP

Published by Paulist Press
997 Macarthur Boulevard
Mahwah, NJ 07430

Printed and bound in the United States of America

# Contents

iv

# Preface

This collection of studies in the theology of Paul the Apostle seeks to set forth some of the important aspects of his mission and his teaching. All of them touch on topics that are of importance to the study of that mission and theology today. Though they may seem disparate at first, they are united by the thrust that they seek to express about Pauline teaching. The studies are intended as further elaborations of topics that I have at times treated all too summarily in my booklet *Paul and His Theology: A Brief Sketch* or in the *NJBC*, art. 79.

Three of these studies (1, 2, 8) are being published here for the first time. The others have appeared in various journals or books. The latter have all been slightly revised for this reprinting of them. My thanks are hereby expressed to the editors of such journals and books who have given permission for the reprinting of these studies here in this revised form.

My thanks are also due to Lawrence Boadt, C.S.P., who accepted this collection of studies for publication by Paulist Press, and to Donald F. Brophy and his staff at Paulist Press for the cooperation that I have had from them in the production of this book.

The original titles of some of the studies have been slightly changed to adapt them to this collection. I list here the original titles and the places where they first appeared:

3. "The Pauline Letters and the Lucan Account of Paul's Missionary Journeys," *Society of Biblical Literature 1988 Seminar Papers* (ed. D. J. Lull; Atlanta, GA: Scholars, 1988) 82–89.

4. "*Abba* and Jesus' Relation to God," *A cause de l'évangile: Etudes sur les Synoptiques et les Actes offertes au P. Jacques Dupont, O.S.B. à l'occasion de son 70ᵉ anniversaire* (LD 123; ed. R. Gantoy; Paris: Cerf; Louvain-la-Neuve: Publications de Saint-André, 1985) 15–38.

5. "Glory Reflected on the Face of Christ (2 Cor 3:7 – 4:6) and a Palestinian Jewish Motif," *TS* 42 (1981) 630–44.

6. "Another Look at *Kephalē* in 1 Corinthians 11:3," *NTS* 35 (1989) 503–11.

7. "The Aramaic Background of Philippians 2:6–11," *CBQ* 50 (1988) 470–83.

Joseph A. Fitzmyer, S.J.
Professor Emeritus, Biblical Studies
The Catholic University of America,
Washington, DC 20064
Resident at the Jesuit Community
Georgetown University,
Washington, DC 20057

ACKNOWLEDGMENTS

The publisher gratefully acknowledges use of the following materials, used with permission: a slightly revised reprint of "The Pauline Letters and the Lucan Account of Paul's Missionary Journeys," by Joseph A. Fitzmyer, S.J., which originally appeared in the *Society of Biblical Literature 1988 Seminar Papers* (Number 27; Atlanta, Georgia: Scholars Press, 1988), pp. 82–89; a slightly revised reprint of "The Aramaic Background of Philippians 2:6–11," by Joseph A. Fitzmyer, S.J., which originally appeared in Vol. 50 (1988), pp. 470–483 of *The Catholic Biblical Quarterly*, The Catholic Biblical Association of America, Washington, D.C.; a slightly revised reprint of "Glory Reflected on the Face of Christ (2 Cor 3:7–4:6) and a Palestinian Jewish Motif," by Joseph A. Fitzmyer, S.J., which originally appeared in Volume 42 (1981) of *Theological Studies*, pp. 630–644; a slightly revised reprint of "Another Look at *Kephalē* in 1 Corinthians 11.3," by Joseph A. Fitzmyer, S.J., which originally appeared in *New Testament Studies*, Volume 35 (1989), pp. 503–511, published by Cambridge University Press; a slightly revised reprint of "*Abba* and Jesus' Relation to God," by Joseph A. Fitzmyer, S.J., which originally appeared in *A cause de l'évangile: Etudes sur les Synoptiques et les Actes offertes au P. Jacques Dupont, O.S.B. à l'occasion de son 70ᵉ anniversaire* (Paris: Cerf, 1985) pp. 15–38.

# Abbreviations

| | |
|---|---|
| AB | Anchor Bible |
| *AD* | G. R. Driver, *Aramaic Documents of the Fifth Century B.C.* (Oxford: Clarendon, 1954) |
| AGSU | Arbeiten zur Geschichte des Spätjudentums und des Urchristentums |
| *AJA* | *American Journal of Archaeology* |
| *AP* | Cowley, A. *Aramaic Papyri of the Fifth Century B.C.* (Oxford: Clarendon, 1923; repr. Osnabrück: Zeller, 1967) |
| ASNU | Acta seminarii neotestamentici upsaliensis |
| ATANT | Abhandlungen zur Theologie des Alten und Neuen Testaments |
| ATD | Das Alte Testament deutsch |
| *b.* | *Babylonian* (followed by name of the tractate of the Talmud) |
| BAGD | W. Bauer, *A Greek-English Lexicon of the New Testament and Other Early Christian Literature* (tr. W. F. Arndt, F. W. Gingrich, and F. W. Danker; Chicago, IL: University of Chicago, 1979) |
| *BCH* | *Bulletin de correspondance hellénique* |
| BETL | Bibliotheca ephemeridum theologicarum lovaniensium |
| *Bib* | *Biblica* |
| BibOr | Biblica et orientalia |

| | |
|---|---|
| *BJRL* | *Bulletin of the John Rylands (University) Library (of Manchester)* |
| BJS | Brown Judaic Studies |
| BKAT | Biblischer Kommentar zum Alten Testament |
| BLA | H. Bauer and P. Leander, *Grammatik des Biblisch-Aramäischen* (Halle/Salle: Niemeyer, 1927) |
| *BMAP* | E. G. Kraeling, *The Brooklyn Museum Aramaic Papyri* (New Haven, CT: Yale University, 1953) |
| BNTC | Black's New Testament Commentaries |
| *CBQ* | *Catholic Biblical Quarterly* |
| CBQMS | Catholic Biblical Quarterly Monograph Series |
| CCLat | Corpus Christianorum, Latin series |
| *CIL* | *Corpus inscriptionum latinarum* |
| *CIS* | *Corpus inscriptionum semiticarum* |
| *DBSup* | *Dictionnaire de la Bible, Supplément* |
| DJD | Discoveries in the Judaean Desert |
| EBib | Etudes bibliques |
| *ESBNT* | J. A. Fitzmyer, *Essays on the Semitic Background of the New Testament* (London: Chapman, 1971; repr. Missoula, MT: Scholars, 1974) |
| *ETL* | *Ephemerides theologicae lovanienses* |
| *EvT* | *Evangelische Theologie* |
| *ExpTim* | *Expository Times* |
| GKC | Gesenius-Kautzsch-Cowley, *Hebrew Grammar* (2d ed.; Oxford: Clarendon, 1910) |
| GCS | Griechische christliche Schriftsteller |
| HNT | Handbuch zum Neuen Testament |
| HNTC | Harper's New Testament Commentaries |
| *HTR* | *Harvard Theological Review* |
| ICC | International and Critical Commentary |
| *IDB* | G. A. Buttrick (ed.), *The Interpreter's Dictionary of the Bible* (4 vols.; Nashville, TN: Abingdon, 1962) |
| *JAAR* | *Journal of the American Academy of Religion* |
| *JBL* | *Journal of Biblical Literature* |
| *JJS* | *Journal of Jewish Studies* |

| | |
|---|---|
| *JQR* | *Jewish Quarterly Review* |
| *JR* | *Journal of Religion* |
| *JSJ* | *Journal for the Study of Judaism in the Persian, Hellenistic and Roman Period* |
| *JSNT* | *Journal for the Study of the New Testament* |
| *JTS* | *Journal of Theological Studies* |
| LD | Lectio divina |
| *Leš* | *Lešonenu* |
| LXX | Septuagint (Greek translation of the Old Testament) |
| *m.* | *Mishnah* (followed by the name of the tractate of the Mishnah) |
| MeyerK | MeyerKommentar (H. A. W. Meyer, *Kritisch-exegetischer Kommentar über das Neue Testament*) |
| *MPAT* | J. A. Fitzmyer and D. J. Harrington, *A Manual of Palestinian Aramaic Texts (Second Century B.C. — Second Century A.D.)* (BibOr 34; Rome: Biblical Institute, 1978) |
| MT | Masoretic Text |
| *NAB* | *New American Bible* |
| NCBC | New Century Bible Commentary |
| *NedTTs* | *Nederlands theologisch Tijdschrift* |
| *NJBC* | R. E. Brown et al. (eds.), *The New Jerome Biblical Commentary* (Englewood Cliffs, NJ: Prentice Hall, 1990) |
| *NovT* | *Novum Testamentum* |
| *NovTSup* | *Supplements to NovT* |
| ns | new series (in any language) |
| *NTA* | *New Testament Abstracts* |
| NTD | Das Neue Testament deutsch |
| *NTS* | *New Testament Studies* |
| NTTS | New Testament Tools and Studies |
| OBO | Orbis biblicus et orientalis |
| *Or* | *Orientalia* |
| *OrAnt* | *Oriens antiquus* |
| *PAHT* | J. A. Fitzmyer, *Paul and His Theology: A Brief Sketch* (2d ed.; Englewood Cliffs, NJ: Prentice-Hall, 1989) |

| | |
|---|---|
| *PL* | J. Migne, *Patrologia latina* |
| *QC* | Qumran Chronicle |
| *RA* | *Revue d'assyriologie et d'archéologie orientale* |
| *RB* | *Revue biblique* |
| *REG* | *Revue des études grecques* |
| *ResQ* | *Restoration Quarterly* |
| *RevQ* | *Revue de Qumran* |
| *RHPR* | *Revue de d'histoire et de philosophie religieuses* |
| *RivB* | *Rivista biblica* |
| *RSV* | *Revised Standard Version* (of the Bible) |
| SANT | Studien zum Alten und Neuen Testament |
| SBLDS | Society of Biblical Literature Dissertation Series |
| *SE II* | *Studia evangelica* (TU 87, 1964) |
| SNTSMS | Studiorum Novi Testamenti Societas Monograph Series |
| *SR* | *Studies in Religion/Sciences religieuses* |
| SSS | Semitic Study Series |
| Str-B | P. Billerbeck, *Kommentar zum Neuen Testament aus Talmud und Midrasch* (6 vols.; Munich: Beck, 1926–63) |
| *TAG* | J. A. Fitzmyer, *To Advance the Gospel: New Testament Studies* (New York: Crossroad, 1981) |
| *TDNT* | G. Kittel and G. Friedrich, *Theological Dictionary of the New Testament* (10 vols.; Grand Rapids, MI: Eerdmans, 1964–76) |
| Tg. | Targum |
| THKNT | Theologischer Handkommentar zum Neuen Testament |
| *TLZ* | *Theologische Literaturzeitung* |
| *TrinJ* | *Trinity Journal* |
| *TS* | *Theological Studies* |
| TU | Texte und Untersuchungen |
| *VD* | *Verbum domini* |
| *VT* | *Vetus Testamentum* |
| *WA* | J. A. Fitzmyer, *A Wandering Aramean: Collected Aramaic Essays* (SBLMS 25; Missoula, MT: Scholars, 1979) |

| | |
|---|---|
| WMANT | Wissenschaftliche Monographien zum Alten und Neuen Testament |
| *ZKT* | *Zeitschrift für katholische Theologie* |
| *ZNW* | *Zeitschrift für die neutestamentliche Wissenschaft* |
| *ZTK* | *Zeitschrift für Theologie und Kirche* |

**Dead Sea Scrolls**

| | |
|---|---|
| CD | Cairo (Genizah) Damascus (Document) |
| 1QapGen | Genesis Apocryphon from Qumran Cave 1 |
| 1QH | *Hôdāyôt* (Thanksgiving Psalms) from Qumran Cave 1 |
| 1QM | *Milḥāmāh* (War Scroll) from Qumran Cave 1 |
| 1QpHab | Pesher of Habakkuk from Qumran Cave 1 |
| 1QS | *Serek* (Manual of Discipline) of Qumran Cave 1 |
| 1QSb | Appendix b of 1QS (Blessings) |
| 1QTLevi | Testament of Levi from Qumran Cave 1 |
| 4Q'Amram[b] | Copy b of 'Amram text from Qumran Cave 4 |
| 4QCatena[a] | Copy a of Catena (String of OT texts) from Qumran Cave 4 |
| 4QEn | Enoch texts from Qumran Cave 4 |
| 4QEnGiants | Enochic Giants texts from Qumran Cave 4 |
| 4QFlor | Florilegium from Qumran Cave 4 |
| 4QJoseph | Joseph text from Qumran Cave 4 |
| 4QMishn | Mishnaic text from Qumran Cave 4 (another name for 4QMMT) |
| 4QMMT | *Miqṣāt ma'ăśê hattôrāh* (Collection of Deeds of the Law) from Qumran Cave 4 |
| 4QOrd | Ordinance text from Qumran Cave 4 |
| 4QpIsa[c] | Copy c of the pesher on Isaiah from Qumran Cave 4 |
| 4QpPs[a] | Copy a of the pesher on the Psalms from Qumran Cave 4 |
| 4QTestim | Testimonia from Qumran Cave 4 |
| 4QTLevi | Testament of Levi from Qumran Cave 4 |
| 4QTQehat | Testament of Qehat from Qumran Cave 4 |
| 6QEnGiants | Enochic Giants text from Qumran Cave 6 |
| 11QtgJob | Targum of Job from Qumran Cave 11 |
| Mur | Murabba'at texts |

# CHAPTER ONE

# The Spiritual Journey of Paul the Apostle

How did Saul of Tarsus become Paul the Apostle? So we might describe the spiritual journey in the life of Paul the Apostle. But it is not a question merely about the change of name for the Apostle of the Gentiles that is recorded in the New Testament. The question is rather asked about how Saul the Pharisee became Paul the Apostle, how Paul the Jew became Paul the Christian.

Before we try, however, to answer the question about Paul's spiritual journey from Pharisaism to Christianity, it might be well to spell out a bit the significance of the names that he bears in the New Testament.

## I. Paul's Name

In his own letters Paul never calls himself Saul, but rather *Paulos,* the name that is used of him also in 2 Pet 3:15, and in the Acts of the Apostles from 13:9 on. Prior to that in Acts his name is *Saulos* (7:58; 8:1,3; 9:1,8,11,22,24; 11:25,30; 12:25; 13:1,2,7), the grecized form of *Saoul,* "Saul." The latter Greek spelling is found only in the conversion accounts, when the risen Christ accosts Paul on the road to Damascus (9:4; 22:7; 26:14) and when Ananias restores his sight (9:17; 22:13). *Saoul* is a Greek transliteration of the Hebrew name of the first king of ancient Israel, *Šā'ûl,* "Saul," as in 1 Sam 9:2,17.[1] This name means "asked" (of God *or* of Yahweh), signifying that the mother had asked of God a child, and the one so named was God's response. Thus Paul's spiritual journey begins even with the Hebrew name given to him by his mother at birth, for he himself recognized that God had set him apart before he was born and called him through his grace (Gal 1:15). Named after Saul, the great king of Israel, Paul had a native background that recalled a rich Jewish heritage. It reveals that Paul's spiritual journey was thus foreseen and destined by God even from his birth.

However, the name that he himself used was *Paulos,* the Greek form of a well-known Roman cognomen (or family name), *Paul(l)us,* used by the Aemilian gens, the Vettenii, and the Sergii.[2] One can only speculate about how Paul got such a Roman name. It is the only thing in his letters that suggests his connection with a Roman background, even if he says nothing in them about his Roman citizenship, of which the Lucan Paul boasts (Acts 22:27-28).[3] Though *paulus* in Latin means "small, little," it really says nothing about Paul's stature or modesty, as is sometimes claimed. It does relate him, however, to a number of famous Roman families.

In the Lucan story the Apostle is at first called Saul, but Acts 13:9 marks the transition, *Saulos de, ho kai Paulos,* "Saul, also known as Paul." From that point on in the Lucan story he is called Paul. This change of names takes place several chapters after the first account of Paul's conversion (Acts 9); so the change had nothing to do with his spiritual conversion.

Moreover, it is sheer coincidence that Saul begins to be called Paul in the episode where the Roman proconsul Sergius Paulus is converted (13:7-12), though some patristic writers have so explained the change of names,[4] suggesting that Paul assumed the name of this illustrious Roman convert from Cyprus.[5]

It is likely, however, that the Apostle was called *Paulos* from birth and that *Saoul* was the "signum" or "supernomen" (added name) used in Jewish circles of the time.[6] For many Jews of the period had two names, one Semitic (like Saul) and the other Greek or Roman (like Paul).[7] The names were often chosen for their similarity of sound.

## II. Paul's Jewish Heritage

The Apostle was keenly aware of himself as a Jew and boasted of his Jewish background, tracing it to descent from Abraham and to the tribe of Benjamin: "I am an Israelite, a descendant of Abraham, a member of the tribe of Benjamin" (Rom 11:1; cf. Phil 3:5; 2 Cor 11:22). As an "Israelite," Paul recognized his privileged status as a member of God's chosen people, "to whom belong the sonship, the glory, the covenants, the giving of the law, the cult, the promises, and the patriarchs," the seven prerogatives that he lists in the paragraph of Romans in which he expresses his sorrow about the condition of his former coreligionists (9:4–5). As a "descendant of Abraham," Paul recognized the value of the status of rectitude in God's sight as a result of the promises made to Abraham and all his offspring (Rom 4:13). As a member of "the tribe of Benjamin," he belonged to the tribe named after the youngest son of Jacob, beloved by his father, and the smallest among all the tribes. It was the tribe from which came Saul, the first king of Israel (1 Sam 9:1,4), after whom the Apostle was named, and from which came Jeremiah, the prophet from Anathoth (Jer 1:1; 32:8).

Paul also boasted of his Pharisaic background: "as to the law a Pharisee" (Phil 3:6), one "extremely zealous for the traditions of my fathers" and one who excelled his peers "in Judaism" (Gal 1:14). The name "Pharisee" probably means "one cut off, set apart" (from Aramaic *pĕrîšāy*), a member of the sect of Palestinian Jews that differed from other Jews and laid great stress on oral tradition or the "oral *tôrāh*" (*tôrāh še-bĕ-'al- pēh*). It was the Jewish sect that considered itself "set apart" from the rest of the Jews (Sadducees, Essenes, and "this rabble that knows not the law" [John 7:49]) because of its strict interpretation of the Mosaic law. Its principle is expressed in the opening paragraph of the Mishnaic tractate *Pirqe Aboth,* "Sayings of the Fathers":

> Moses received the law from Sinai and entrusted it to Joshua, and Joshua to the elders, and the elders to the prophets; and

the prophets entrusted it to the men of the Great Synagogue. They said three things: Be deliberate in judgment, raise up many disciples, and make a fence around the law.[8]

To be "deliberate in judgment" meant to interpret the law of Moses strictly; to "raise up many disciples" meant to proselytize; and to "build a fence around the law" meant to guard the written *tôrāh* with the oral interpretation inherited from the traditions of the Fathers. This was the sect of Jews, then, that was influenced by the Hellenistic ideal of virtue as *aretē,* "excellence," and believed that it could produce a holy and virtuous people by instruction and education in the Mosaic *tôrāh.*

This Pharisaic background may well explain what Paul meant when he says of himself in Romans that he was "set apart for God's gospel" (1:1). In other words, he may have been playing on the name "Pharisee" and looking on his Pharisaic background, his training as "one set apart," as divinely ordained. For it prepared him to become a preacher of God's gospel. Yet it is ironic that that gospel should turn out to be, not a proclamation of strict observance of "the deeds of the law" (Rom 3:20) in the Pharisaic sense, but of justification by grace through faith "apart from deeds of the law" (Rom 3:28), apart from that which meant so much to the Pharisee of his day.

There is a paradox in all of this, since many of the items that seem so characteristically Jewish in his letters and even sloganlike, echoing what seem like typical phrases that one would tend to ascribe to his Pharisaic background, are now known to be associated more with Essene tenets than with Pharisaic. (See further chap. 2.)

Apart from such a Pharisaic or other Jewish background to the spirituality of Paul, however, one otherwise notes that Paul lives in the world of the Judaism of the Old Testament. His God is the God of his fathers, the God of "the old dispensation" (2 Cor 3:14), who spoke through the prophets, and indeed, who announced his gospel beforehand in the prophets (Rom 1:2).

Paul thinks and expresses himself in Old Testament categories and makes abundant use of Old Testament images, quotations, and allusions. He cites the Old Testament more than 90 times.[9] Though he usually quotes the Old Testament according to the Greek Septuagint, his use of it is similar to that of the authors of contemporary Jewish writings or other intertestamental literature.[10] Even his introductory clauses or phrases, when he cites the Old Testament explicitly, are consonant with Jewish practice, even if they are closer to those of Qumran writings than to the Mishnaic.[11]

Paul does not quote Scripture as one would in the twentieth century, but his mode is close to that of contemporary Jewish writers. He may accommodate the Old Testament or give it new meaning (e.g., when he announces his theme about salvation by faith and quotes Hab 2:4 in Rom 1:17 or Gal 3:11); he may allegorize it (e.g., when he make use of the story of Sarah and Hagar and quotes Gen 16:15 or 17:16 in Gal 4:21-25); or he may wrest it from its original context (e.g., when he quotes Deut 25:5 about not muzzling the ox that treads the threshing floor and applies it to Christian preachers in 1 Cor 9:9). In such use he is no different from contemporary Jewish writers.

Yet he does quote the Old Testament to stress the unity of God's action in both dispensations. He looks upon the Old Testament as God's way of preparing for the gospel or preparing for Christ himself (Gal 3:24). Even if he contrasts the "letter [of the law] and the Spirit" (2 Cor 3:6), the Old Testament is still for him the means whereby God speaks to humanity, as he recognizes in Rom 4:23-24, when he acknowledges that what was written about Abraham is still relevant to Christians; cf. Rom 15:4. Indeed, most of Paul's teaching about God, his *theo*logy, is clearly derived from his Jewish background, echoing in many respects the Old Testament itself.

Yet he is also a Jew of the first century, influenced by *various* currents of Jewish thinking that are now evident from the post-Old Testament world. In any case, we see that Paul's spiritual journey is rooted in his native Judaism.

### III. Paul's Cultural Heritage

The spiritual journey of Paul has to take into consideration not only Paul's Jewish background, but also his cultural heritage. For he was not a Jew of Palestine. Though Luke makes Paul assert that he was brought up in Jerusalem and educated at the feet of Gamaliel (Acts 22:3), his letters never give an indication of the influence of Palestinian Judaism, apart from some points to be discussed in chapter 2. Indeed, part of the paradox is just how the Pharisaic and other Jewish influence, rooted in Palestine, came to affect so markedly a Jew of the diaspora.

Paul's Roman name, his quotation of the Old Testament in Greek and usually according to the LXX, his composition of his letters in Greek reveal his diaspora background, for he was also a child of the Greco-Roman world. His call and conversion were an experience that took place outside of Judea, near Damascus, an important town in Hellenized Syria. If the Lucan tradition is correct that he was a Jew of Tarsus, "a citizen of no mean town" (Acts 21:39), its cultural heritage too would have rubbed off on him. For Tarsus was a city in the ancient world famed for its intellectual and pedagogic tradition. It was accorded the status of a free city in the Roman empire by Mark Antony in 66 B.C., when it was made the capital of the province of Cilicia. In the first century B.C. it had become the seat of a famous school of philosophy.

Paul called himself "a Hebrew" (Phil 3:5), by which he probably meant that he was a Greek-speaking Jew who also spoke Aramaic.[12] That language, however, was widely used in his day throughout Syria and Asia Minor, so that it does not really speak against influence from the Hellenistic world in which Paul would have spent his youth. His writings reveal that he had been liberally educated in the Hellenistic tradition of the time.

Even if Paul had not been trained as a Greek *rhētōr,* his mode of composition and expression often reveals the influence of Greek rhetoric and Greek education. Traces of the Cynic-Stoic mode of argumentation called *diatribē* are found in his letters: a mode of discourse conducted in familiar, conversational style and developed by lively debate with an imaginary interlocutor; its sentence structure is often short, and questions are interjected; antitheses and parallel phrases often punctuate the development (see Rom 2:1–20; 3:1–9; 1 Cor 9).[13]

Even more, his style and his mode of composing letters have been analyzed. They reveal that many of the contemporary modes of Greek rhetorical argument are found in them, especially in his letters to the Galatians and to the Romans.[14] The rhetorical elements are important indications of the careful argumentation that Paul has made use of in order to present his gospel and his understanding of Christ and his significance for humanity.

Whereas Jesus' illustrations often reflect the agrarian life of Galilee, Paul frequently uses images derived from urban culture and Hellenistic ambience. He uses Greek political terminology (Phil 1:17; 3:20), alludes to Greek games (Phil 2:16; 1 Cor 9:24–27), employs Greek commercial terms (Phlm 18) or legal terminology (Gal 3:15; 4:1–2; Rom 7:1), and refers to Hellenistic slave trade (1 Cor 7:22; Rom 7:14) or Hellenistic celebrations in honor of a visiting emperor (1 Thess 2:19). He employs the Hellenistic ideas of *eleutheria,* "freedom" (Gal 5:1,13), *syneidēsis,* "conscience" (1 Cor 8:7,10,12; 10:25–29; 2 Cor 5:11; Rom 2:15), and the Stoic ideas of *autarkeia,* "sufficiency, contentment" (2 Cor 9:8), or *physis,* "nature" (Rom 2:14).

This Greek cultural background eventually enabled Paul, the diaspora Jew, to cope with the problems and difficulties of carrying the Christian gospel from its Palestinian Jewish matrix into the world of the Roman empire. But his experience in that world too as the Apostle of the Gentiles also contributed to his spiritual journey. For he not only carried the gospel to the eastern Mediterranean world of his day, but also founded churches and Christian communities in this Hellenistic milieu. His practical experience and concrete contacts with diaspora Jews and with Gentiles of that area had a significant impact on his view of Christianity. Would Paul have written about justification as he did, if he had not coped with the problem of Jewish converts to Christianity in the diaspora trying to insist with Gentile converts that they too had to observe the Mosaic law to be saved? The universal scope of Christian salvation undoubtedly dawned on Paul as he worked continually with Jews who failed to accept his gospel and with Gentiles who did heed his message. Though from his earliest letters he reveals an awareness of the privileged position of his fellow Jews in God's plan of salvation (1 Thess 2:13–14; cf. Rom 1:16; 2:9–10), he eventually had to wrestle explicitly with that problem (Romans 9–11). He admits that he has been "indebted to Greeks and to Barbarians" (Rom 1:14).

Moreover, the church as "the body of Christ" (1 Cor 12:27-28) is almost certainly the result of his understanding of the Christian *ekklēsia* in the light of the contemporary Greco-Roman idea of the state as the body politic.[15] This notion would, then, have come to him, not as a result of his experience on the road to Damascus, but rather as a result of his missionary experience in the eastern Mediterranean world of the time.

Such were the Hellenistic influences on Paul of Tarsus, a diaspora Jew called by God to announce his gospel to the Gentiles.

## IV. Paul's Call to Be an Apostle

The most important element in the spiritual journey of Paul was the experience that he had on the road to Damascus. That experience was a revelation made to him about Christ Jesus, and his faith in the risen Christ developed from that experience. It was not merely a psychological "conversion" that could be explained in terms of Paul's Jewish background, or even in terms of what he writes in Romans 7. That chapter has often been interpreted as an autobiographical description of Paul himself, as a young Jewish boy reaching puberty and coming to an awareness of what the law would mean in his life; hence, crushed by the law's demands, he would have been freed by conversion to Christ. Such an interpretation of Romans 7, however, does not do justice to the obvious universal situation of humanity confronted by law that is depicted there. For even as a Christian, Paul was able to look back on his Pharisaic past and say of it that "as to righteousness under the law" he had been "blameless" (Phil 3:6). He did not look back, even as a Christian, at his Jewish past as one of failure to cope with the demands of the Mosaic law, under which he lived.

Paul himself speaks of that experience near Damascus as a revelation of the Son accorded to him by the Father (Gal 1:16); in it he "saw Jesus the Lord" (1 Cor 9:1; cf. 1 Cor 15:8). That revelation of the crucified "Lord of glory" (1 Cor 2:8) not only summoned Paul the Pharisee to become an apostle, but made of him the first Christian theologian. The only difference between that appearance of the risen Christ to him (1 Cor 15:8) and those to the official witnesses of the resurrection (1 Cor 15:5-7) was that his experience occurred much later, and to him as an individual. But it did put him on an equal footing with the Twelve and others to whom the risen Christ had appeared. In defending his right to be recognized as an "apostle," which was apparently contested in the early church by those who knew that he had not witnessed the earthly ministry of Jesus, he exclaimed, "Am I not an apostle? Have I not seen Jesus our Lord?" (1 Cor 9:1). Paul spoke of his call as an event in which he had been "seized" by Christ Jesus (Phil 3:12), and as a "necessity" (or compulsion), which had been laid upon him to preach the gospel to the Gentiles (1 Cor 9:16; cf. Gal 1:16b). He compared that experience to God's initial creation of light: "For God who said, 'Let light shine out of darkness,' has shone in our hearts to give us the light of the knowledge of God's glory on the face of Christ" (2 Cor 4:6).

Thus the compulsion of divine grace pressed Paul into the service of Christ and his gospel. His response to that call was one of vivid faith, in which he confessed with the early church that "Jesus is Lord" (1 Cor 12:3; cf. Rom 10:9; Phil 2:11). In a creative act, God illumined the mind of Paul and gave him an insight into what a later disciple of Paul would call "the mystery of Christ" (Eph 3:4).

We can sum up the effects of that experience on Paul in three ways: (1) That "revelation" (Gal 1:12,16) impressed Paul with the unity of divine action for the salvation of all humanity, which is manifest in both the Old and the New Dispensations. As a result of that encounter with the risen Christ, Paul did not become a Marcionite, rejecting the Old Testament. The Father who revealed his Son to Paul was the same God that Paul the Pharisee had always worshiped and served. He was the creator, the lord of history, the God who continually saved his people Israel, and who proved to be a faithful lord of the covenant despite Israel's infidelities. The experience near Damascus did not alter Paul's basic commitment to the "one God."

(2) That vision instructed Paul in the soteriological value of the death and resurrection of Jesus the Messiah in God's salvific plan. If Paul's basic *theo*logy did not change, his *christo*logy did. As a Jew, Paul shared the messianic expecta-

tions of his people (see Dan 9:25; cf. 1QS 9:11, where Palestinian Jews were said to be awaiting the coming of a prophet [like Moses, Deut 18:15-18] and Messiahs of Aaron and Israel). He had looked forward to the coming of a messiah (of some sort). But the vision accorded to him near Damascus taught him that God's Anointed One had already come, that he was "Jesus our Lord, who was handed over (to death) for our offenses and raised for our justification" (Rom 4:25). Before his experience near Damascus, Paul certainly knew that Jesus of Nazareth had been crucified, "hung on a tree," and hence "cursed" by the very law that Paul himself had so zealously observed (Gal 3:13; cf. 1:14). But that revelation impressed on him the messianic, soteriological, and vicarious value of the death of Jesus in a way that he never suspected before. With a logic that only a Pharisee could appreciate, Paul saw Christ Jesus taking upon himself the law's curse and transforming it into its opposite, so that Christ became the means of freeing humanity from malediction. The cross, which had been the stumbling block to Jews, became in his eyes "the power and the wisdom of God" (1 Cor 1:24). Henceforth, Paul would understand that crucified "Lord of glory" (1 Cor 2:8) as his exalted Messiah.

(3) That revelation also impressed Paul with a new vision of salvation history. Before the encounter with the Lord, Paul saw human history divided into great periods: (i) from Adam to Moses (the period without the law [Rom 5:14a]); (ii) from Moses to the Messiah (the period of the law [Rom 5:14b]); (iii) the messianic age (the period when the law would be perfected, fulfilled, or even done away with). The experience near Damascus, however, instructed Paul that the messianic age had already begun; it thus introduced a new perspective into salvation history. The *eschaton,* "endtime," so anxiously awaited before, had already been started; the ages had met (1 Cor 10:11), although a definite stage of the last age or newly inaugurated *eschaton* was still to be realized (as was hoped, not too far in the future). The Messiah had come, but not yet in glory. Paul realized that he (with all Christians) thus found himself in a double situation: one in which he looked back upon the death and resurrection of Jesus as the inauguration of the

new age, and another in which he still looked forward to Christ's coming in glory, to his parousia.

Thus, far more than Paul's Pharisaic background, or even his Hellenistic cultural roots, the revelation of Christ on the road to Damascus gave Paul an ineffable insight into "the mystery of Christ." It enabled him to fashion his "gospel," to preach the fundamental good news of salvation in a form that was distinctively his own. But Paul did not immediately understand all the implications of the vision granted to him. It provided only a basic insight that was to color all that he was to learn about Jesus and his mission among human beings, not only from the early church's tradition that preceded him, but also from his own apostolic activity in preaching "Christ crucified" (1 Cor 1:23).

Thus that experience on the road to Damascus was a turning-point in Paul's spiritual journey. It made of him not only an "apostle of the Gentiles" (Rom 11:13), but a founder of Christian communities, an interpreter of the Christ-event, and the first Christian theologian whose interpretation we have inherited. It was a turning-point, because Paul's career did not end with that experience. Thereafter, as a result of his preaching, his founding of churches, and his writing of letters to the churches in various places, he continued to grow in the knowledge of Christ Jesus. He learned to interpret the effects of what Christ Jesus had done for humanity in his passion, death, resurrection, exaltation, and heavenly intercession. In other words, he learned to interpret the various effects of the Christ-event.

## V. The Effects of the Christ-Event
### As Seen by the Mature Apostle

When Paul looked back at the Christ-event, he saw it as a complex unit, something like a ten-sided solid figure. When he gazed at a panel of it from one direction, he said that Christ "justified" us; when he gazed at it from another, he said that Christ "saved" us; or from another, Christ "transformed" us, and so on. In other words, Paul made use of images drawn from his Jewish or Hellenistic background to describe what was really indescribable. In doing so, he made use of ten different images or figures:

(1) *Justification.* Christ Jesus "justified" us; he brought it about that all sinful human beings might stand before God's tribunal acquitted or vindicated, that they might stand before him as righteous persons. Thus Paul drew upon his Jewish background (Deut 25:1; Ps 7:9–12) and derived from it the image of justification as an effect of the Christ-event. What Jews of old sought to achieve in God's sight by observing the deeds of the law, Christ Jesus by his death and resurrection brought about for all sinners, Jews and Greeks alike. In his experience near Damascus Paul realized the truth that all human beings have sinned and have failed to attain the share of divine glory destined for them, but also that that share was now achievable through what Christ Jesus had obtained for them vicariously (Rom 3:21–26). Thus, Paul realized that the righteousness that he and other Christians have is not their own; it is a "righteousness from God" (Phil 3:9; cf. Rom 10:3), a gift freely bestowed by God because of what Christ Jesus has done for humanity. God thus became for Paul the source of life "in Christ Jesus," because God had made him "our righteousness" (1 Cor 1:30), the means whereby Paul himself became upright or righteous.

(2) *Salvation.* Christ Jesus "saved" us; he has delivered us from evil (from physical harm, psychic harm, cataclysmic evil, and moral evil); he has restored us to a status of wholeness in the sight of God. Thus Christians "are being saved" by the cross of Christ (1 Cor 1:18,21). Salvation as an effect of the Christ-event has not yet been wholly achieved, for it still has an eschatological aspect (1 Thess 2:16; 5:8–9; 1 Cor 3:15; Rom 5:9–10). That is why Paul tells the Philippians, "work out your own salvation in fear and trembling" (2:12), adding, however, immediately, "for God is the one working in you, both to will and to work for his good pleasure" (2:13), lest anyone think that salvation can be achieved without God's grace. Thus Paul realized that his own salvation depended on what God by his grace had wrought in him because of the death and crucifixion of Christ Jesus.

(3) *Reconciliation.* Christ Jesus has "reconciled" us with the Father; he has altered our relationship with God, changing our

status from one of hatred, enmity, and hostility to one of love, friendship, and intimacy. Again, the initiative lies in God himself, for through Christ he has drawn us from alienation to peace and intimacy with himself. Thus, Christ has made us *to be at one* with God; he has atoned us (Rom 5:10–11). Moreover, this effect of the Christ-event also has its cosmic effect, because "God was in Christ, reconciling the world (the *kosmos*) to himself" (2 Cor 5:18–19). Thus Paul makes use of a social-politic image drawn from his Hellenistic background to express yet another effect of the Christ-event. Moreover, he applies it not only in an anthropological sense, but also in a cosmic sense. He sensed that his own spiritual journey had been advanced by this Christic reconciliation and atonement.

(4) *Expiation.* Christ Jesus has "expiated" our sins; he has wiped away the sins of humanity. For through the death of his son and the shedding of his blood, the Father has publicly displayed Christ Jesus as the new Mercy-Seat. What the sprinkling of the ark of the covenant with the blood of animals by the high priest each year on *Yôm Kippûr* symbolized for Israel (Lev 16:14–20), that Christ Jesus has obtained for all humanity by his own blood and by his death (Rom 3:25). Thus, Paul has again derived from his Jewish background yet another image to explain an effect of the Christ-event. He thus became aware of the significance of the death of Jesus in the expiation of his own sins and how that death contributed to his own progress in his dedication of his life to the service of God and his gospel.

(5) *Redemption.* Christ Jesus has "redeemed" us; he has ransomed us from bondage to evil and enslavement to sin. For Christ has become "our redemption" (1 Cor 1:30). Again, Paul sees this effect of the Christ-event as also having eschatological and cosmic aspects, for "through the redemption which is in Christ Jesus" (Rom 3:24), Christians "await the redemption of the body" (Rom 8:23), and all (physical) "creation" is groaning in expectation of that event (Rom 8:19–22). It is not easy to determine whence Paul has derived this image; it may be drawn from his Hellenistic background, the Greco-Roman world in which slavery and emancipation were commonly practiced. But it may also be drawn from the Old Testament idea of Yahweh as *gô'ēl*, "redeemer," acquiring his people as he freed

them from Egyptian bondage (Isa 41:14; 43:14; 44:6; 47:4; Ps 19:15; 78:35). Paul himself recognized that in his spiritual journey he too had enjoyed this emancipation brought about by God through Christ Jesus.

(6) *Freedom.* Christ Jesus has "freed" us; he has given Christians the rights of citizens in a free city; he has made them citizens of heaven: "our commonwealth is in heaven" (Phil 3:20), i.e. the real Christian homeland, a stake in the life that the risen Christ himself enjoys in the glorious presence of the Father. Again, this image is derived from Paul's Hellenistic background, from the world that knew of cities and states and that enjoyed "freedom" in the Roman empire. Paul not only exhorted the Galatians to "stand fast in that freedom with which Christ has made your free" (Gal 5:1), but he knew that his own spiritual journey shared in this liberated status, "Am I not free?" (1 Cor 9:1).

(7) *Sanctification.* Christ Jesus has "sanctified" us; he has dedicated us to the awesome service of God, thus marking off Christians from the profane and the secular to engage them in the awesome worship and praise of the heavenly Father. So Christ has become "our sanctification" (1 Cor 1:30; cf. 1 Thess 4:7), i.e. the means whereby human beings may be so dedicated. This image Paul has derived from his Jewish background, which spoke of the sanctification of persons and objects, dedicating them to the service of Yahweh in his Temple (Isa 48:2; 64:10; Exod 19:14; Lev 19:2). Paul personally was aware of such service, for he compared his own preaching of the gospel to the liturgical or cultic act of the priests who served in the Jerusalem Temple (Rom 1:9). Thus his own spiritual journey included the evangelization of the Gentiles and the priestly offering of them to God as "sanctified by the Spirit" (Rom 15:16).

(8) *Transformation.* Christ Jesus has "transformed" us; he has gradually reshaped those human beings "who turn to the Lord" so that they behold the glory of the Lord and are "transformed into a likeness of him from one degree of glory to another" (2 Cor 3:18). Paul explains how the face of the risen Christ has become a mirror reflecting the glory coming from the creator God: "It is the God who said, 'Let light shine

out of darkness,' who has shone in our hearts to give us the light of the knowledge of God's glory on the face of Christ" (2 Cor 4:6). This is the most sublime of the effects of the Christ-event that Paul has sketched for us. He has not hesitated to derive from his Hellenistic background an image used in Greek mythology, because even such a rich image could aptly express what for Paul was the magnificent calling of the Christian. As the caterpillar is transformed into the butterfly, Paul himself was transformed; from the Pharisaic Jew he became the Christian apostle of the Gentiles. Greek patristic writers often used this Pauline idea in developing their teaching about the *theōsis,* "divinization," of the Christian.[16]

(9) *New Creation.* Christ Jesus has "created" us "anew"; what God did at the beginning of all things, that Christ Jesus has done again in a new way (Gal 6:15; 2 Cor 5:17). He has given us "newness of life" (Rom 6:4), and because Christ has given us a share in his risen life, he has become "the last Adam" (1 Cor 15:45), i.e., the Adam of the *eschaton,* the Adam of the endtime, the head of a new humanity. Again, Paul has derived this idea from the Old Testament teaching about the creator God. He realized that in his spiritual journey he too had become part of this new humanity. His Adamic existence had become a Christic existence.

(10) *Glorification.* Christ Jesus has "glorified" us; he has made it possible to attain "the glory of God," of which all sinful human beings had fallen short (Rom 3:23). "Those whom he [God] predestined he also called; and those whom he called he also justified; and those whom he justified he also glorified" (Rom 8:30). Here Paul has taken another image from the Old Testament, the "glory" (Greek *doxa,* Hebrew *kābôd*) as the sign of the presence of God to his people or his world. He now sees Christ Jesus obtaining for Christians access to the glorious presence of the Father that he already enjoys as of his resurrection. For the destiny of the Christian is "to be always with the Lord" (1 Thess 4:17), i.e. to share in the risen Lord's own life and existence in the Father's presence. Paul debated with himself, as he lay in prison, whether it would be better for him to be freed to continue his evangelization or to die and "be with Christ" (Phil 1:23): "For to me to live is Christ, to die is gain"

(1:21). Thus he envisaged the goal of his spiritual journey, to share in the glory of the risen Christ, the goal for which the Father had predestined him.[17]

So Paul summed up in a striking way the effects of the Christ-event and their bearing on his own spiritual journey. He has thereby made us understand the heights that he himself attained in his journey. In his attempt to formulate for Christians of all generations what Christ Jesus has achieved for them, he has revealed the road that he himself had travelled.

We can do no better than terminate this discussion of Paul's spiritual journey than to quote his own reaction to it all:

> Would that you would bear with me in a little foolishness! Do bear with me! I feel a divine jealousy for you, for I betrothed you to Christ to present you as a pure bride to her one husband. But I am afraid that, as the serpent deceived Eve by his cunning, your thoughts will be led astray from a sincere and pure devotion to Christ. For if some one comes and preaches another Jesus than the one we preached, or if you receive a different spirit from the one you received, or if you accept a different gospel from the one you accepted, you submit to it readily enough. I think that I am not in the least inferior to those superlative apostles. Yet even if I am unskilled in speaking, I am not in knowledge; in every way we have made this plain to you (2 Cor 11:1-6).

Paul himself realized that the spiritual journey that he had made in his life and ministry of preaching Christ crucified resulted in a "knowledge" that was not inferior to that of those whom some people regarded as "apostles" superior to himself. Paul again battled with those who refused to recognize him as their equal, as one on a par with the Twelve. He had not been a member of the Twelve, for he had not witnessed the ministry of Jesus himself. Yet he turned out to be a superior proclaimer of Christ crucified. For, as he says,

> I must boast; there is nothing to be gained by it, but I will go on to visions and revelations of the Lord. I know a man in Christ who fourteen years ago was caught up to the third heaven — whether in the body or out of it I do not know, God knows. And I know that this man was caught up into Paradise — whether in the body or out of the body I do not know, God knows — and he heard things that cannot be told, which no one may utter. On behalf of this man will I boast; but on my own behalf I will

not boast, except of my weaknesses. . . . But God said to me, "My grace is sufficient for you, for my power is made perfect in weakness" (2 Cor 12:1–9).

This, then, is the height to which the Apostle Paul travelled in his spiritual journey. He was made perfect by Christ's grace, despite the weaknesses that he himself experienced in his ministry of preaching Christ crucified. He had journeyed far ("from Jerusalem all the way around to Illyricum," Rom 15:19) and labored hard to become not only "the Apostle of the Gentiles" (Rom 11:13), but an "ambassador for Christ" (2 Cor 5:20), led in triumph by Christ, who has spread the fragrance of the knowledge of God everywhere (2 Cor 2:14).

# CHAPTER TWO

# Paul's Jewish Background and the Deeds of the Law

In his letter to the Philippians Paul of Tarsus boasted of his Jewish background: "circumcised on the eighth day, of the people of Israel, of the tribe of Benjamin, a Hebrew born of Hebrews; as to the law a Pharisee, as to zeal a persecutor of the church, as to righteousness under the law blameless" (3:5-6). In his Second Letter to the Corinthians he asserted, "Are they Hebrews? So am I!" (11:22). Again, in Gal 1:14 he insists that he outstripped "in Judaism" many of his own age among his people: "so zealous was I for the traditions of my fathers."[1] We may recall too the sorrow that he expressed in Rom 9:1 for the lot of his former coreligionists.

The same Pharisaic background is attributed to Paul by Luke in Acts 22:3, when he presents Paul maintaining that he was educated at the feet of Gamaliel, who in Acts 5:34 is said to be a Pharisee, a member of the council. Again in Acts 23:6, when Luke depicts Paul maintaining before the Sadducees and the Pharisees in the Sanhedrin, "I am a Pharisee, a son of Pharisees"; and in Acts 26:5 when he portrays Paul asserting before King Agrippa, "I have lived as a Pharisee according to the strictest party of our religion."[2] Thus both Paul himself and Luke have stressed the Apostle's Pharisaic background.

Now despite such affirmations of Paul and Luke, R. Bultmann felt constrained to explain Paul's historical position thus: "*Paul originated in Hellenistic Judaism.*"[3] Though Bultmann accepted Luke's testimony about Paul's home being Tarsus

(Acts 9:11; 21:39; 22:3), he questioned the correctness of Paul as a pupil of Gamaliel; instead, he insisted that Paul *"was won to the Christian faith by the kerygma of the Hellenistic Church."*[4] "His letters barely show traces of the influence of Palestinian tradition concerning the history and preaching of Jesus."[5] Such a view, however, raises the question about Paul's connections with the "Palestinian tradition" of Judaism, traces of which are certainly found in his writings, and even in a more pronounced way than traces of mystery religions or gnosticism.[6]

The issue is complicated. Part of the problem is that we cannot simply predicate of pre-70 Palestinian Judaism that picture of Pharisaism that one derives today from the rabbinic sources, which were eventually codified under Rabbi Judah the Prince ca. A.D. 200.[7] And yet the "traditions of my fathers" that Paul speaks of in Gal 1:14 are something that he knows about as characteristic of the kind of "Judaism" to which he belonged. He knows that those traditions were different from *hē graphē,* "Scripture" (Rom 9:17; 10:11) or *hai graphai hagiai,* "the holy Scriptures" (Rom 1:2). Thus Paul was aware of a form of the Palestinian Pharisaic distinction of the written and the oral law, even though he may not have spoken or written about *tôrāh še-biktāb,* "the law that is in writing," and *tôrāh še-bě-'al peh,* "the law that is according to the mouth," the later rabbinic way of expressing the distinction. Yet this awareness did not come to him from his Hellenistic background alone.[8] Paul's writings, indeed, may reflect at times such a Palestinian Pharisaic background, but there is more to be said.

The strange thing about it is that, now that we know a bit more about Judaism in pre-70 Palestine, echoes of another sort of Judaism are also found in Pauline writings. This, then, says something about the Jewish background of which Paul boasted. In what follows I should like to concentrate on (I) the Jewish background of *ta erga tou nomou;* (II) other evidence of a different Palestinian Jewish influence on Paul's theology; and (III) an attempt to identify this other influence.

## I. The Deeds of the Law

Given Paul's Jewish background, and especially his own affirmations about his pre-Christian past as a Pharisee, one might expect that the phrase frequently used by him, *(ta) erga (tou) nomou,* "(the) deeds of (the) law" (Gal 2:16; 3:2,5,10; Rom 2:15; 3:20,28), or in its abbreviated form, *ta erga* (Rom 3:27; 4:2,6; 9:11,32; 11:6) would have come from Pharisaism. It is a phrase that sounds like a slogan derived from his Jewish theological background, summing up the deeds prescribed or proscribed in the Mosaic Law, its "precepts." Yet when one looks for the Jewish background of such a slogan, one finds it neither in the Old Testament itself nor in the writings of the Pharisaic-rabbinic tradition. Billerbeck openly admitted that "the old rabbinic literature has no expression that formally corresponds to *erga nomou. Erga nomou* would be in Hebrew *ma'ăśê tôrāh* or in Aramaic *'ubdê 'ôrāytā';* but these expressions are unknown to the rabbinic sages."[9] It is, indeed, striking that this Pauline slogan-like phrase seems to have been foreign to the Pharisaic-rabbinic tradition.[10]

Yet the Hebrew equivalent has turned up in Qumran literature from Palestine itself. When J. M. Allegro first published the text that he called 4QFlorilegium,[11] he did not include among the fragments an important part of the text. Later, when he published more of the fragmentary text,[12] he included lines 6-7: *wyw'mr lbnwt lw' mqdš 'dm lhywt mqṭyrym bw' lw' lpnyw m'śy twrh,* "and he proposed to build for Him a man-made sanctuary in which deeds of the law might be performed in his presence (as) sacrifices to Him."[13] Allegro called attention in a footnote of his *JBL* article to Paul's use of *ergon/a (tou) nomou* in Galatians and Romans, but omitted all mention of the Pauline parallel in the official publication of the text in DJD 5.

When J. Strugnell wrote a lengthy critical review of Allegro's publication,[14] he questioned Allegro's reading of *ma'ăśê tôrāh* and suggested reading instead *ma'ăśê tôdāh,* "deeds of thanksgiving" ("avec dalet endommagé").[15] If Strugnell's reading were correct, then the Hebrew equivalent of the Pauline phrase would have disappeared from this Qumran text. But, in my opinion, a glance at plate XIX reveals that Allegro has read the phrase correctly, *ma'ăśê tôrāh;* the letter is *resh,* not *daleth.* This reading is, moreover, supported by a passage in 1QS 6:18, which speaks of "the Many" in the community, who scrutinize a candidate who would join the community *'l dbryw lpy śklw wm'śyw btwrh,* "concerning his words according to his insight and his deeds in the law" (i.e. in the observance of the law). (See also 1QS 5:21,23; 6:14; CD 13:11.)[16]

Again, in 1QpHab 7:11, "men of fidelity" are described as *'wśy htwrh,* "doers of the law."[17] The same phrase occurs again in 1QpHab 8:1; 12:4; 4QpPs[a] 1-2 ii 14,22.[18] A significant variant of the phrase is found in 11QTemple 56:3: *w'śyth 'l py htwrh,* "and you shall do according to the law."[19]

Moreover, E. Qimron and J. Strugnell have recently reported that there is a text of Qumran Cave 4 that they are preparing for publication, and the title they have given to it is *mqṣt m'śy htwrh,* "some of the deeds of the law" (4QMMT).[20] It is preserved in six copies (4Q394-99), all very fragmentary, but supplementary to each other. One of the fragments is dated palaeographically to the mid-second century B.C.[21] The text contains a letter from a leader in the Qumran community, possibly the Teacher of Righteousness himself, to the leader of Jews who are outsiders and disagree with him. The letter apparently had four parts: (a) an introduction (now completely lost); (b) a calendar (partly preserved); (c) a list of over twenty *halakhot,* each one of which begins, *w'p 'l X 'nḥnw 'wmrym š-,* "and concerning X we say that . . ."; (d) an epilogue, which discusses the sect's reasons for withdrawal from the rest of the people. Now in this epilogue the phrase *mqṣt m'śy htwrh,* clearly appears, showing that Allegro's reading of *m'śy twrh* was correct.

1. [    ]*w 'wnwt zkwr* [*'t*] *dwyd šhw' 'yš ḥsdym* [*w*]*'p*
2. *hw'* [*n*]*ṣl mṣrwt rbwt wnslwh lw w'p 'nḥnw ktbnw 'lyk*
3. *mqṣt m'śy htwrh šḥšbnw lṭwb lk wl'mk š*[    ]
4. *'mk 'rmh wmd' twrh hbn bkl 'lh wbqš mlpnw*
5. *'t 'ṣtk whrḥyq mmk mḥšbwt r'h w'ṣt bly'l*
6. *bšl štśmḥ b'ḥryt h't bmṣ'k mqṣt dbrynw kn*
7. *wnḥšbh lk lṣdqh b'śwtk hyšr whṭwb lpnw lṭwb lk*
8. *wlyśr'l.*

1. [    ] iniquities. Remember David, that he was a pious man and also (that)
2. he was delivered from many afflictions, and pardon was granted him. Moreover, we have written to you (about)

3. some of the precepts of the law, which we consider for your welfare and that of your people, because w[e recognize] (that)
4. you have prudence and knowledge of the law. Be wise in all these (things) and seek from Him
5. your good counsel that He may keep far from you evil plots and the scheming of Belial,
6. so that you may rejoice at the end of time, as you find some of our words (are) right.
7. It will be reckoned to you as righteousness, as you do what is upright and good before Him for your welfare
8. and (that) of Israel.

It is clear, therefore, that *m'śym* is to be understood as "precepts" and that the verb *'śy* means "to perform" deeds prescribed by the law. In Exod 18:20 the noun *m'śh* is used in reference to observance of the law: *wĕhizhartāh 'ethem 'et-haḥuqqîm wĕ'et-hattôrāh wĕhôda'tā lāhem 'et-hadderek yēlĕkû bāh wĕ'et-hamma'ăśeh 'ăšer ya'ăśûn*, "enlighten them in regard to the statutes and the law, showing them the way they are to walk and the deeds they are to do." This becomes in Tg. Onqelos, *wĕtazhar yātĕhôn yāt qayyāmayyā' wĕyāt 'ôrāyātā' ûtĕhôda' lĕhôn yāt 'ôrāytā' dîhākûn bah wĕyāt 'ubādā' dĕya'bĕdûn*, "you shall enlighten them about the covenants and the laws, and you shall make known to them the law by which they must walk and the deed(s) that they shall do."[22] In these instances the Hebrew verb *'śy* or the Aramaic verb *'bd* is used in the sense of "doing" or "performing" the deeds prescribed by the law. Thus the use of *'śy* in Exod 18:20 provides an Old Testament background for the Pauline expression "deeds of the law," even though the exact phrase itself is never found in these Scriptures. The verb *'śy* is also found with *ḥuqqîm*, "statutes" or with *miṣwôt*, "commandments" (e.g. Num 15:39; Deut 16:12; 30:8).

It should also be noted how in this Qumran text "righteousness" (*ṣdqh*, line 7) is associated with "deeds of the law," precisely in the way that Paul makes use of the slogan.

This evidence now bears in an important way on the Pauline usage. For the meaning of Paul's phrase was often queried and debated.[23] For instance, the meaning of Paul's phrase *ta erga tou nomou* has been used as a slogan to emphasize that no one can fulfill the law as it requires, or again, that it serves only a legalistic end, advocating that righteousness can be attained by meritorious deeds, or as Bultmann would have put, by idolatrous efforts. It has recently been restricted by J. D. G. Dunn to mean *"particular observances of the law like circumcision and the food laws,"* i.e. those observances *"widely regarded as characteristically and distinctively Jewish."*[24] In this view Paul would be attacking a "basic Jewish self-understanding."[25] According to Dunn, such "works of the law" are regarded neither by Paul nor by his Jewish interlocutors as "works which *earn* God's favour, as merit-amassing observances. They are rather seen as *badges:* they are simply what membership of the covenant people involves, what mark out the Jews as God's people."[26]

Yet it is now seen in the light of this Qumran text that "works of the law" cannot be so restricted. The text of 4QMMT does single out about twenty halakhot, but they are not limited to circumcision and food laws; they are moreover associated by the Jewish leader who wrote this letter with the status of "righteousness" before God. There are, indeed, food regulations among the precepts singled out, but they include many others, e.g. regulations about sacrifices, about the impurity of members, tithes to be paid, etc. In fact, it makes explicit mention of study of "the Book of Moses and the words of the prophets and David." Given such a broad outlook, it is difficult to see how the restriction of the phrase that Paul uses can be understood in Dunn's sense.

From this Qumran text it is made clear that the sloganlike phrase did indeed have a legalistic connotation and that it was used in connection with the way a Jew would seek for righteousness in God's sight. That is precisely the point that the leader makes in his letter.

Similarly, it is difficult in light of the use of this expression in 4QMMT to accept the meaning of the Pauline phrase "works of the law" as a subjective genitive, as proposed by L. Gaston.[27] He would mean by it that the law actually works, i.e. "the law actively works in the Gentile world to create a situation from which we need redemption."[28]

Moreover, the sense of the phrase as used in 4QMMT raises the question why Paul's expression should reflect such a Palestinian Jewish background, not Pharisaic, but different. Indeed, Paul himself reproaches the Jews, "It is not those who hear the law who are righteous in the sight of God, but those who do it (*hoi poiētai nomou*) who will be justified" (Rom 2:13).

## II. Other Evidence of a Different Palestinian Jewish Background

This is, of course, not the only instance of such Palestinian non-Pharisaic Jewish influence in Paul's writings. We may gather together other evidence of a different Jewish influence under the following six headings:

(1) Various modern authors have noted the similarity of Paul's teaching on the sinfulness of all humanity and on justification itself as something that reflects a Palestinian sectarian understanding.

Though Paul himself as a Christian could look back on his Jewish past and could boast of it as one in which he was "blameless as to righteousness under the law" (Phil 3:5), yet his experience near Damascus impressed him with the sinfulness of all human beings and with the role of Christ Jesus in rectifying that status. Thus he came in time to assert the sinfulness of all humanity, himself included. "All have sinned and fall short of the glory of God" (Rom 3:23); "yet we [Jewish Christians, like Peter and Paul] know that no human being is justified by works of the law, but through faith in Christ Jesus" (Gal 2:16). In this idea Paul was echoing, but also sharpening, what was already the teaching of the Old Testament itself in Psalms 51, 103, and 143. But what the Old Testament there taught was filtered to him through the awareness of contemporary Palestinian Jewish teaching such as we now detect in, for instance, the Qumran *Manual of Discipline:* "As for me, I belong to wicked humanity, to the assembly of perverse flesh; my iniquities, my transgressions, my sins together with the wickedness of my heart belong to the assembly doomed to worms and walking in darkness" (1QS 11:9–10).[29]

Again Paul's teaching about *dikaiōsis,* "justification," as an effect of the Christ-event, is also derived from his Old Testament and Jewish background. It expresses a rectified relationship between God and human beings or between human beings themselves, whether as kings or commoners, brothers or sisters, or neighbors. It connotes a societal, but above all a judicial relationship, either ethical or forensic (i.e., related to law courts: see Deut 25:1; cf. Gen 18:25). It was a difficult status for a Jew to achieve in the sight of God (Job 4:17; 9:2; Ps 143:2). Josephus could imagine nothing "more righteous" than obeying the statutes of the Law (*Ag.Ap.* 2.41 §293) to achieve that status of rectitude before God the Judge. Yet the sectarians of Qumran also sang of their sinfulness and sought justification only from God:

> No human being sets his own path or directs his own steps, for to God alone belongs the judgment of him, and from His hand comes perfection of way. . . . If I stumble because of a sin of the flesh, my judgment is according to God's righteousness. If He unleashes distress on me, from the Pit He will draw back my soul and establish my footsteps in the way. In His mercy He has drawn me close (to Him), and with His favors will He render judgment of me. He has judged me in His righteous fidelity; in His bounteous goodness He expiates all my iniquities, and in His righteousness He cleanses me of human defilement and of human sinfulness, that I may praise God for His righteousness and the Most High for His majesty. (1QS 11:10–15)

> Who can stand righ[te]ous before You when he is judged? No answer can be made to Your judgment! All (human) glory is (like the) wind, and no one is able to stand before Your wrath. Yet all Your faithful children You bring to pardon before You, [to clean]se them of their transgressions with much goodness and in the abundance of Your me[r]cy. (1QH 7:28–30)

> [Your hand] has [gui]ded me unto this day, and Your righteousness judges my [si]ns, but Your peaceful protection is set to save my soul; and over my steps is much pardon, and an abundance of [mer]cy, when You exercise judgment of me (1QH 9:32–34).

> For You are righteous, and all Your chosen ones (stand for) fidelity. You will destroy forever all iniquity [and e]vil. Your righteousness will be revealed in the sight of all that You have made. Through the abundance of Your goodness have I come to know and I have established with an oath on my soul to sin

against You no more [and to] do nothing that is evil in Your sight (1QH 14:15-18).

As for me, I know that righteousness does not belong to a human being, nor perfection of way to a son of man. To God Most High belong all deeds of righteousness, whereas the path of a human is not set firm, unless (it be) by the spirit (which) God has fashioned for him . . . And I said, It is because of my transgression that I have been abandoned far from Your covenant. But when I recalled Your mighty hand along with the abundance of Your mercy, then I was restored and I stood up; my spirit strengthened my stance against blows, because [I] have based myself on Your graces and on the abundance of Your mercy. For You expiate iniquity to clean[se a human b]eing from guilt by Your righteousness. (1QH 4:30-37)[30]

Here we find an awareness both of sin's pervasiveness and of God as the source of human righteousness that provides a transition between the Old Testament teaching about God judging humanity with righteousness (Ps 9:9) or the postexilic idea of God acquitting the sinner in a just but righteous judgment (Isa 46:13; 51:5,6,8), and the Christian, especially the Pauline, understanding of justification. The difference between the sectarian and the Pauline teaching on justification is that Paul emphasizes that this grace is an effect of the Christ-event apprehended by humans through faith: "by his grace as a gift" (Rom 3:24, *dōrean tē autou chariti*), and "by faith" (Rom 3:25, *dia tēs pisteōs*). "By grace" and "through faith in Christ Jesus" (Rom 3:22) are the Pauline specifications added to the early Christian teaching about Christ as our righteousness (1 Cor 1:30) that he may have inherited.[31] Thus did Paul specify at least the *mode* of justification.

(2) We have to relate Pauline teaching on predestination to the Qumran sectarian conviction. In Rom 8:30 Paul writes, "Those whom he predestined he also called; and those whom he called he also justified; and those whom he justified he also glorified."[32] Though the Pharisaic-rabbinic tradition did speak of the divine foreknowledge of Adam, the Torah, Israel, Abraham's ram, the name of the Messiah, etc.,[33] it did not develop a formal teaching about the predestination of human beings, such as one finds in Qumran literature.[34] Here the idea of predestination is clearly set forth:

From the God of knowledge is all that is and will be, and before they came to be He established all the design of them. As they come into being they fulfill their tasks according to what has been determined for them in His glorious design, without any change. In His hand lie the decisions for all things. He upholds them in all their needs. He it is who made man to rule over the world. He allotted him two spirits in which to walk until the time of His visitation: these are the spirits of truth and perversity. The origin of truth is from a fountain of light; the origin of perversity is from a fountain of darkness. Dominion over all the sons of righteousness is in the hand of the Prince of Light; they walk in the paths of light. All dominion over the sons of perversity is in the hand of the Angel of Darkness; they walk in the paths of darkness. The straying of all the sons of righteousness is because of the Angel of Darkness; all their sin, their iniquities, their fault(s), and the transgression of their deeds are because of his dominion according to the mysteries of God until His end-time. (1QS 3:15–23)[35]

In this regard Paul's thinking and mode of speaking clearly reflect such a Palestinian Jewish background.

(3) Attempts have been made at times to trace the Pauline idea of *mystērion* to Paul's Hellenistic background.[36] True, in the rites of some mystery religions of the time the initiate was brought into relationship with the deity through a vision (*epopteia*) and was assured of salvation (*sōtēria*) through the protection of the deity. In Pauline writings, however, the idea of *mystērion* bears only a superficial verbal resemblance to such Hellenistic ideas, since the content of his *mystērion* is quite different.[37] It bears, indeed, on salvation that is brought to human beings, but it is really closer to the idea of *rāz,* "secret," used in Dan 2:18,19,27, etc., where it denotes the content of a dream or a divine revelation made to a king that has to be interpreted.

For Paul it denotes a secret hidden in God for ages and now made known to humanity in Christ Jesus that the salvation available to human beings comes through Christ; it shares in the apocalyptic character of *euangelion,* "gospel." Thus in 1 Cor 2:1–2 Paul equates "God's mystery" with "Jesus Christ . . . crucified,"[38] just as he had equated the "gospel" with "Christ crucified" (1 Cor 1:17,23–24). Indeed, Paul regarded himself as a "steward" dispensing the wealth of this mystery (1 Cor 4:1).

Now it is this notion of mystery that has again turned up in the Qumran literature. In the commentary on Habakkuk we read, apropos of Hab 2:2:

¹*wydbr 'l 'l hbqwq lktwb 't hb'wt 'l* ²{'*l*} *hdwr h'hrwn w't gmr hqs lw' hwd'w* ³*w'šr 'mr lm'n yrws hqwr' bw,* ⁴*pšrw 'l mwrh hsdq 'šr hwdy'w 'l 't* ⁵*kwl rzy dbry 'bdyw hnb'ym.*

And God told Habakkuk to write down the things that were to come to pass in the last generation, but the end of time he did not make known to him. As for what it says, 'that one may read it on the run,' the explanation of it concerns the Teacher of Righteousness to whom God made known all the mysteries of the words of his servants the prophets. (1QpHab 7:1-5)

Here one sees *rz* meaning something hidden in God that is now made known; in this idea one finds the parallel to Paul's *mystērion.* The content of the "mystery" is different. In the Qumran commentary it refers to the hidden meaning of God's words to the prophet Habakkuk,[39] whereas in Pauline theology the content of the mystery is Christ and his role in salvation now made known.[40] What is the same in both the Qumran and the Pauline usage is the idea of *mystērion* or *rāz* as a *carrier,* whereas the content or what is carried is different.

(4) As a designation of Christian disciples Paul uses the expression *huioi phōtos,* "sons of light" (1 Thess 5:5). Though the counterpart *huioi skotias,* "sons of darkness," is not found in his writings, or anywhere else in the New Testament, the phrase echoes a peculiarly dualistic way of thinking. The figurative use of *huios* is a Septuagintism.[41] The pair, "light" and "darkness," is attested, indeed, in the Old Testament as a symbol of ethical good and evil, weal and woe (Ps 112:4; Isa 42:6-7; 45:7; 59:9-10; Job 29:3; Prov 4:18-19; Mic 7:8),[42] but the Semitic phrase used to distinguish all humanity into two groups as "sons of light" or "sons of darkness" is not found in the Old Testament or in later rabbinic literature.[43] Yet it has turned up often in Qumran literature as a favorite way of designating members of the sectarian community, being used both in Hebrew (*běnê 'ôr,* 1QS 1:9; 2:16; 3:13,24,25; 1QM 1:3,9,11,13; 4QFlor 1-2 i 8-9; 4Q177 10-11:7; 12-13 i 7,11) and in Aramaic (*běnê něhôrā',* 4Q'Amram^b 3:1). In such

writings one also finds the counterpart, "sons of darkness" in Hebrew (*běnê ḥôšek*) and Aramaic (*běnê ḥăšôkā'*), the designation for Jews who were not members of the community. It is thus striking that Paul's designation of Christian disciples makes use of an anarthrous Semitic-sounding phrase *huioi phōtos* that is the exact Greek counterpart of such a Palestinian sectarian Jewish locution.[44] The dualism that is found in Qumran writings is of an ethical sort, subordinated to Jewish monotheism, and has nothing to do with a Hellenistic background.[45]

(5) We may also cite the mode in which Paul introduces the explicit quotations of the Old Testament used in his letters.[46] For instance:

(1) *kathōs gegraptai*, "as it has been written" (Rom 1:17; 2:24; 3:4, 10; 4:17; 8:36; 9:13,33; 10:15; 11:8,26; 15:3,9,21; 1 Cor 1:31; 2:9; 2 Cor 8:15; 9:9). This formula is found in the LXX (2 Kgs 14:6; 23:21; 2 Chr 23:18; Dan 9:13 [Theodotion]); its Hebrew equivalent would be *k'šr ktwb* (used in 1QS 5:17; 8:14; CD 7:19; 4QFlor 1-2 i 12; 4QpIsaᶜ 4-7 ii 18; 47:2; 4QCatenaᵃ 10-11:1; 4Q178 3:2), which is also used in the Masoretic text of the Old Testament (1 Kgs 21:12; Dan 9:13). Cf. 11QMelch 9.

(2) *hōsper gegraptai*, "as it is written" (1 Cor 10:7).

(3) *houtōs gar/kai gegraptai*, "for/and thus it is written" (1 Cor 15:45); such a formula is not found in the LXX, but has its exact equivalent in the Qumran Hebrew phrase *ky kn ktwb* (1QS 5:15; CD 11:18; 2Q25 1:3).

(4) *kata to gegrammenon*, "according to what has been written" (2 Cor 4:13).

(5) *en tō nomō gegraptai*, "it is written in the law" (1 Cor 14:21), introducing a quotation not from the Pentateuch but from Isa 28:11! Compare LXX 2 Kgs 14:6 (*kathōs gegraptai en bibliō nomōn*); 23:21; but also 4QFlor 1-2 i 2,15 (*k'šr ktwb bspr* [*mwšh*].

(6) *en gar tō Mōyseōs nomō gegraptai*, "for it is written in the law of Moses" (1 Cor 9:9), which is somewhat similar to the foregoing Qumran phrase (4QFlor 1-2 i 2; cf. 4QpIsaᶜ 1:4). Compare LXX 2 Chr 23:18 (*kathōs gegraptai en nomō Mōysē*).

(7)    *gegraptai gar* or *hoti gegraptai,* "for it is written" (Rom 12:19; 14:11; 1 Cor 1:19; 3:19; Gal 3:10,13; 4:27 [in Gal 4:22 it occurs without an explicit quotation!], which is the Greek equivalent of Hebrew *ky ktwb* (CD 11:20).

(8)    *kata to eirēmenon,* "as it is said" (Rom 4:18); cf. the Qumran phrase *k'šr 'mr* (CD 7:8 [= 19:5],14,16; 20:16; [13:23].

(9)    *prōtōs Mōysēs legei,* "first Moses says" (Rom 10:19); cf. 4QOrd (4Q159) 5:7, [*k'š*]*r dbr mwšh,* "[a]s Moses said"; cf. CD 5:8. *kai Daueid legei,* "and David says" (Rom 11:9); cf. 4QCatena^a 12–13 i 2, *'šr 'mr Dwyd,* "which David said." *Esaias gar legei,* "for Isaiah says" (Rom 10:16,20; 15:10; 16:12); cf. CD 6:7–8, *'šr 'mr yš'yh,* "as Isaiah said." *pros de ton Israēl legei* [*Esaias*], "and about Israel (Isaiah) says" (Rom 10:21); *Esaias de krazei hyper ton Israēl,* "Isaiah cries out about Israel" (Rom 9:27); cf. CD 8:14; 19:26–27, *'šr 'mr mwšh lyšr'l,* "what Moses said to Israel." *hōs kai en tō Hōsēe legei,* "as he even says in Hosea" (Rom 9:25).

(10)   *kathōs kai ho nomos legei,* "as even the law says" (1 Cor 14:34 [without introducing a quotation of the law!].

(11)   *kathōs eipen ho theos,* "as God said" (2 Cor 6:16). Cf. the Qumran phrase *'šr 'mr 'l,* "as for what God said" (CD 6:13; 8:9); or *'l 'šr 'mr lw,* "God who said to him" (CD 9:7); or *w'šr 'mr,* "as for what he [God] said" (11QMelch 2,[3],10,11,[14],15[bis], 18,19,26).

(12)   *legei gar hē graphē,* "for Scripture says" (Rom 9:17; 10:11). Or *tí gar hē graphē legei,* "for what does Scripture say?" (Rom 4:3); or *ouk oidate en Elia tí legei hē graphē,* "do you not know what Scripture says in (the passage about) Elijah?" (Rom 11:2).[47]

Now what is striking about these introductory formulas is that, although they use the verbs "write" and "say" as do the formulas in the later rabbinic tradition of the Mishnah, the actual formulas in the Qumran literature are much different from the Mishnaic. Years ago B. M. Metzger made a comparative study of the formulas used to introduce the Old

Testament quotations in the Mishnah and the New Testament.
"By far the majority of quotations in the Mishnah are introduced by the verb *'mr.*"[48] The forms of the verb most frequently
used are the participle *'wmr* and the niphal *n'mr* (or *šn'mr*),
with some other variations. But there is not one formula in
Metzger's list that corresponds to anything in my list constructed
from the Qumran texts.[49] The Mishnah also uses the root *ktb*
in both nominal and verbal forms, but not one of the examples
listed by Metzger parallels any of the usages of the Qumran
literature. This reveals, then, that Paul's introductory formulas,
which have far more parallels to the Qumran formulas than
to the Mishnaic, imitate a contemporary Palestinian mode of
quoting Scripture. This raises the question, therefore, Why is
the Pauline mode of introducing Old Testament quotations
closer to the Qumran sectarian mode than to the Pharisaic-
rabbinic mode of the Mishnah? Can the mode have so radically
changed from the pre-70 Palestinian custom to that of the
Mishnaic in the course of some 150 years? Or is a different
custom being followed?

(6) A comparison can be made with the Pauline use of
*testimonia* lists and the Qumran text 4QTestimonia. Paul uses
such a literary device in Rom 3:10–18 (to show that all have
sinned); 15:9–12 (to show that the heathen praise the God of
Israel); 9:25–29. In his careful study of Paul's use of the Old
Testament, O. Michel remarked that there existed no *testimonia*
collections in Jewish tradition.[50]

> There are no traces of pre-Christian *florilegia,* neither of the
> late Hellenistic Jewish type (Hatch), nor of the late rabbinical
> sort (Vollmer). Moreover the hypothesis of R. Harris, that there
> were early Christian *florilegia,* which would have been composed
> prior to the writings of the New Testament, cannot be regarded
> as probable. Collections of that sort occur first in an early
> Christian setting; they can be proved to exist with Melito of
> Sardis and Cyprian. Probably their origin can be traced to an
> even earlier time; the Epistle of Barnabas perhaps supposes
> them. But the impression we get is that the Gentile Christian
> Church compiled these *florilegia* for missionary and polemical
> purposes.[51]

Such a *testimonia*-list or *florilegium* has turned up in Qumran
literature. J. M. Allegro published 4QTestim in 1956.[52]

According to Allegro, it strings together quotations of Deut 5:28–29; 18:18–19 (referring to a prophet like Moses); Num 24:15–17 (an oracle of Balaam, referring to a star coming from Jacob and a scepter from Israel); Deut 33:8–11 (referring to Levi); and 4QPsJosh (a commentary on Josh 6:26). Allegro suggested that the unifying theme was eschatological, i.e., the destruction of those who did not accept the teaching of the Qumran sect. The lineup of Old Testament texts also suggested that the list was made to illustrate the sect's messianic beliefs about a coming prophet, a Messiah of Israel, and a Messiah of Aaron (1QS 9:11), to which was appended a quotation from the Psalms of Joshua, invoked against the sect's enemies. But P. W. Skehan showed that the first quotation (said to be from Deut 5:28–29 and 18:18–19) was actually a quotation in one paragraph and similar to that of Exod 20:21b according to a proto-Samaritan text-tradition.[53] Thus the order of the texts would suggest rather citations from Bible in its normal order (Exodus, Numbers, Deuteronomy, Joshua). Moreover, according to CD 7:18–20 the star in the oracle of Balaam is interpreted as a (or the) priest; and the scepter as a Davidic royal Messiah. Hence the threefold citation may not be intended as messianic. Yet in either case, whether intended to be messianic or eschatological, the text does preserve a *testimonia*-list of some sort. It thus provides a Palestinian Jewish antecedent to the *testimonia*-lists of the Pauline letters. Again, it is noteworthy that this device, unknown to the Pharisaic-rabbinic tradition, has turned up to be in use in the Qumran sect's writings.

Undoubtedly, still other items could be added to the foregoing list of Pauline ideas that have been found to have counterparts in these sectarian Jewish writings. What does one make of them? The parallels are there, and we may be misled by parallelomania. Years ago S. Sandmel warned us of this danger.[54] Again, one often sees quoted the famous dictum of E. R. Goodenough about literary parallels: a parallel by definition consists of straight lines in the same plane which never meet, however far they are extended in any direction. But the definition is derived from mathematics and applied to literature. To repeat the dictum as if it closes the discussion or absolves one from investigating the literary relationship of authors is only a form of obscurantism, something little better than parallelomania or pan-Qumranism. It may even enable one to avoid asking the question when a *literary* parallel might cease to be such and actually prove to be a "contact."

The problem remains, How does one explain such parallels or contacts in the Pauline literature and such a Palestinian Jewish corpus, given what Paul himself says about his Pharisaic Jewish background and what we know today about such a tradition in the rabbinic writings inherited from that background. Perhaps Paul's Jewish background was more diverse than we realize.[55]

### III. An Attempt to Identify
### This Other Influence

Though scholars have at times sought to identify the Qumran sect with a variety of ancient Jews, the most commonly accepted identification has been the Essene hypothesis. The Essenes are not mentioned in the New Testament, but they are one of the three sects among the Jews of ancient Palestine recognized by Flavius Josephus.[56] His description of the Essenes has been studied in detail and many of the characteristics of them that he mentions have been illustrated by texts from Qumran. T. S. Beall has recently devoted a monograph to such a comparison, *Josephus' Description of the Essenes Illustrated by the Dead Sea Scrolls.*[57]

But now, on the heels of such a discussion, there appear the articles of E. Qimron and J. Strugnell that begin to upset that hypothesis, because it seems that 4QMMT may be a text stemming from, not an Essene, but a Sadducean background. Though we have to await the full publication of this document before a certain judgment can be made, there are already discussions of it that are pushing in that direction. Qimron and Strugnell themselves have recognized that

> two or three of the halakhot on ritual purity expressed in our work are cited also in early Rabbinic literature as the opinion of the Sadducees in their controversies with the Pharisees. MMT thus becomes an important piece of evidence in establishing the identity of the Sadducees (and Boethusians) mentioned in Rabbinic sources.[58]

We are confronted, however, by a cardinal problem when we compare between Josephus's description of the aristocratic non-strict Sadducees and the *halakhot* ascribed to the Sadducees in the Talmud, for they do not tally. It has been suggested that the talmudic use of the name Sadducees was extended to encompass divergent sects, not only Josephus's aristocratic one. How can MMT serve to clarify the identification of these ancient sects? In MMT there are three *halakhot* on questions cited in talmudic sources as topics of controversy between Sadducees and the Pharisees. In all three cases, MMT is identical in view with that of the Sadducees in the Talmud. Further similar instances in the Qumranic literature were noted long ago by the late S. Liebermann. This strengthens the opinion of those scholars who hold that the name "Sadducees" (and apparently also "Bethusians") in the talmudic sources generally refers to such extremist sects as the Dead Sea Sect.[59]

In a similar way L. H. Schiffman, who has had access to the manuscript of the book which Strugnell and Qimron are publishing on 4QMMT, writes:

> In the 20 or so disputes listed in this text, the view ascribed by the letter to the opponents of the emerging sect is usually the same as that attributed in rabbinic literature to the Pharisees or the tannaim [mishnaic rabbis]. In those cases where tannaitic texts preserve the corresponding Pharisee-Sadducee conflicts regarding the same matters discussed in Miqṣat Ma'aseh Ha-Torah, the view espoused by the writers of this document is that of the Sadducees. Only one possible explanation can be offered for this phenomenon. The earliest members of the sect must have been Sadducees who were unwilling to accept the situation that came into being in the aftermath of the Maccabean revolt (168–164 B.C.E.).[60]
> . . . we see the Sadducees of Josephus as the *ṣdoqim* of rabbinic literature, who, it is turning out, are closely related to the *bene ṣadoq* ("Sons of Zadok") who apparently founded the Dead Sea sect.[61]

Now such a view is intriguing, but is it right? It is impossible at this time to judge whether this hypothesis of Qimron, Strugnell, and Schiffman is correct. Once the text of 4QMMT itself is published officially and we can see how it is explained, it will be possible to study further the ramifications of this proposal. For it runs counter not only to what Josephus says about the Sadducees, as Qimron and Strugnell have recognized, but also to what the New Testament says about the Sadducees, who according to Acts 23:8, "say that there is no resurrection, nor angel, nor spirit; but the Pharisees acknowledge them all." How one is going to reconcile all the Qumran data about predestination, angels, the afterlife with what is thus otherwise known from ancient sources about the Sadducees is going to be a major problem.[62]

But there are already voices that are protesting the hypothesis of Qimron, Strugnell, and Schiffman. J. M. Baumgarten has already shown that there are at least seven problems in Qumran law that militate against such a hypothesis.[63] Similarly, J. C. VanderKam has listed some of the difficulties with this identification of the Qumran sect.[64]

In any case, whether the Qumran sect be identified with the Essenes or the Sadducees, the image that is emerging is the difference of them from the Pharisees. Then how explain the similarities of the various Pauline material that we have gathered above with the ideas of the Qumran sect? If the Qumran sect were, indeed, Sadducean, then the Palestinian Jewish background of Paul the Apostle would become even more complicated than if it were Essene. At any rate, that background remains a puzzle in view of what he himself has told us about his Jewish heritage. But it also instructs us about how little we really know about the diversity of Judaism in the first centuries B.C. and A.D. Moreover, it complicates considerably our thinking about Paul's acknowledged Pharisaic background, and about his connections with Palestinian Judaism. Where and how would he have come into contact with this non-Pharisaic Palestinian Judaism, which some of the items in his theological teaching echo?

# CHAPTER THREE

# The Pauline Letters
# and the Lucan Account
# of Paul's Missionary Journeys

Recent studies of Paul's letters and the chronology of his missionary journeys have rightly insisted that one must give priority to the evidence about his apostolic movements in his own letters, especially the uncontested seven letters (1 Thessalonians, Galatians, Philippians, 1–2 Corinthians, Romans, and Philemon).[1] At the same time some of these studies have expressed a negative or at least a somewhat pejorative attitude toward the Lucan account of Paul's apostolic journeying. There is room, however, for another look at the relationship between the evidence of Paul's letters and the Lucan account of his journeys, especially since some of the recent studies eventually admit a bit of the Lucan data into their consideration of the Pauline evidence. For instance, J. Murphy-O'Connor agrees that Paul's appearance before the proconsul L. Junius Gallio in Achaia (Acts 18:12) is the "one link between the Apostle's career and general history that is accepted by all scholars."[2] And yet, that appearance before Gallio is known to us only from the Lucan account. The upshot is that the use of Lucan data for the reconstruction of Pauline chronology is somewhat arbitrary, and the account of the so-called first missionary journey in Acts is often dismissed or regarded with distrust. Clearly, the Lucan data have to be scrutinized critically, but my impression is that more of the Lucan materials could be used than is usually done; hence my attempt to reconsider certain aspects of them here.

The Lucan account of Paul's apostolic movements in Acts is structured in three blocks. Modern students of Pauline chronology often cite the comment of John Knox about this threefold division of Pauline missionary journeys: "If you had stopped Paul on the streets of Ephesus and said to him, 'Paul, which of your missionary journeys are you on now?' he would have looked at you blankly without the remotest idea of what was in your mind."[3] True, but the difficulty comes not solely from the structure of the Lucan story in Acts, but much more from the way modern readers have read Acts, since Luke has not distinguished Mission I, II, or III or counted them as we have learned to do.

It is not my intention to work out a complete defense of the Lucan story of Paul's missionary journeys. Rather, I should like to discuss critically three aspects of the problem that the Lucan materials present in the reconstruction of the life of Paul, emphasizing what I consider support from the Lucan story for the evidence that we actually have in Paul's own letters. I acknowledge the priority of the Pauline evidence and recognize that it not only takes precedence over the Lucan data but that the latter have to yield, if and when there is a conflict or hesitation about the relationship. The three aspects are the following: (I) the correlation that exists in the Pauline and Lucan materials; (II) the problem of Mission I (before the so-called Council); and (III) the appearance of Paul before Gallio in Achaia.

### I. The Correlation That Exists
### in the Pauline and Lucan Materials

In 1955 T. H. Campbell wrote an article that, in my opinion, deserves much more attention than it has been accorded. In "Paul's 'Missionary Journeys' as Reflected in His Letters,"[4] Campbell showed that in Paul's uncontested letters there is a sequence of movement from his experience on the road near Damascus to his (projected) arrival in Rome that more or less parallels the detailed movements in the Lucan story of Acts.[5] The principal passages about personal details in the Pauline letters are the following: 1 Thess 2:1-2,17-18; 3:1-3a,6; Gal

1:13–23; 2:1–14; 4:13; Phil 3:5–6; 4:15–16; 1 Cor 1:11; 4:17; 5:9; 7:7–8; 15:32; 16:1–10,12,17; 2 Cor 1:8,15–16,19; 2:1,9–13; 7:5–6; 9:2–4; 11:7–9,23–27,32–33; 12:2–4,14,21; 13:1–2,10; Rom 11:1c; 15:19b,22–32; 16:1.

In the chart that follows I adapt Campbell's fundamental comparison of items in the Pauline letters with similar items in Acts, making use of added data that have emerged in recent discussions and adding references to some of Paul's collaborators.

| *Letters* | *Acts* |
|---|---|
| Conversion/Call near Damascus (implied in Gal 1:17c) | Damascus (9:1–22) |
| To Arabia (Gal 1:17b) | |
| Return to Damascus (1:17c):3 years | |
| Flight from Damascus (2 Cor 11:32–33) | Flight from Damascus (9:23–25) |
| To Jerusalem (Gal 1:18–20) | To Jerusalem (9:26–29) |
| To "the regions of Syria and Cilicia" (Gal 1:21–22) | Caesarea and Tarsus (9:30) |
| | Antioch (11:26a) |
| | (Jerusalem [11:29–30; 12:25]) |
| | Mission I: Antioch (13:1–4a), Seleucia, Salamis, Cyprus (13:4b–12) |
| Churches evangelized before Macedonia (Philippi, Phil 4:15) | South Galatian towns (13:13–14:25) |
| | Return to Antioch (14:26–28) |
| "Once again during 14 years I went up to Jerusalem (for "Council," Gal 2:1) | Jerusalem (15:1–12) |
| Antioch Incident (Gal 2:11–14) | Antioch (15:35; Mission II) |
| | Syria and Cilicia (15:41) |
| | South Galatia (16:1–5) |
| Galatia (1 Cor 16:1) evangelized for the first time (Gal 4:13) | Phrygia and North Galatia (16:6) |

Philippi (1 Thess 2:2 [=Macedonia, 2 Cor 11:9])
Thessalonica (1 Thess 2:2; cf. 3:6; Phil 4:15-16)

Athens (1 Thess 3:1; cf. 2:17-18)
Corinth evangelized (cf. 2 Cor 1:19; 11:7-9)
Timothy arrives in Corinth 1 Thess 3:6), probably accompanied by Silvanus (1 Thess 1:1)

Apollos (in Ephesus) urged by Paul to go to Corinth (1 Cor 16:12)

Northern Galatia, second visit (Gal 4:13)
Ephesus (1 Cor 16:1-8)

Visit of Chloe, Stephanas et al. to Paul in Ephesus (1 Cor 1:11; 16:17), bringing a letter (7:1)
Paul imprisoned (? cf. 1 Cor 15:32; 2 Cor 1:8)
Timothy sent to Corinth (1 Cor 4:17; 16:10)
Paul's second "painful" visit to Corinth (2 Cor 13:2); return to Ephesus

Mysia and Troas (16:7-10)
Philippi (16:11-40)

Amphipolis, Apollonia, Thessalonica (17:1-9)
Beroea (17:10-14)
Athens (17:15-34)
Corinth for 18 months (18:1-18a)
Silas and Timothy come from Macedonia (18:5)

Paul leaves from Cenchreae (18:18b)
Leaves Priscilla and Aquila at Ephesus (18:19-21)
Apollos dispatched to Achaia by Priscilla and Aquila (18:17)
Paul to Caesarea Maritima (18:22a)
Paul to Jerusalem (18:22b [implied])
In Antioch for a certain time (18:22c)
Mission III: North Galatia and Phrygia (18:23)
Ephesus for 3 yrs. or 2 yrs., 3 mos. (19:1-20:1; cf. 20:31)

| | |
|---|---|
| Titus sent to Corinth with letter "written in tears" (2 Cor 2:13) | |
| (Paul's plans to visit Macedonia, Corinth, and Jerusalem/Judea [1 Cor 16:3–8; cf. 2 Cor 1:15–16]) | (Paul's plans to visit Macedonia, Achaia, Jerusalem, Rome [19:21]) |
| Ministry in Troas (2 Cor 2:12) | |
| To Macedonia (2 Cor 2:13; 7:5; 9:2b–4); arrival of Titus (2 Cor 7:6) | Macedonia (20:1b) |
| Titus sent on ahead to Corinth (2 Cor 7:16–17), with part of 2 Cor | |
| Illyricum (Rom 15:19)? | |
| Achaia (Rom 15:26; 16:1); Paul's third visit to Corinth (2 Cor 13:1) | 3 mos. in Greece (Achaia, 20:2–3) |
| | Paul starts to return by boat to Syria (20:3), but goes instead via Macedonia and Philippi (20:3b–6a) |
| | Troas (20:6b–12) |
| | Miletus (20:15c–38) |
| | Tyre, Ptolemais, Caesarea Maritima (21:7–14) |
| (Paul plans to visit Jerusalem, Rome, Spain [Rom 15:22–27]) | Jerusalem (21:15–23:30) |
| | Caesarea Maritima (23:31–26:32) |
| | Journey to Rome (27:1–28:14) |
| | Rome (28:15–31)[6] |

The most important differences in the preceding correlation of Pauline and Lucan data are the following: (1) Luke seems to know nothing about Paul's withdrawal to Arabia after his experience near Damascus (Gal 1:17b). (2) Luke treats Paul's missionary endeavors in three blocks (I: 13:1–14:28; II: 15:36–18:22; III: 18:23–21:16). (3) Whereas Paul himself in 2 Cor 11:32–33 relates his departure from Damascus to the attempt of the ethnarch of King Aretas IV Philopatris to take him captive, Luke ascribes the departure to a plot of "the Jews" to kill him (Acts 9:23). (4) Whereas Paul himself speaks only of having persecuted "the church of God" (Gal 1:13) or "the church" (Phil 3:6), Luke portrays Paul "consenting" to the stoning of Stephen (Acts 7:58–8:1), about which Paul says nothing in his letters, and further pursuing men and women belonging to "the Way" as far as Damascus to bring them to prison (Acts 8:3). But apart from these important differences, the correlation of the rest of the Pauline and Lucan data is significant. The biggest difficulty in the consideration of it is the Lucan account of Mission I, to which we now turn.

## II. The Problem of Mission I
### (before the so-called Council)

The end of the Lucan account of Saul's conversion or call in Acts 9 tells of his escape from Damascus (vv. 24–25), his coming to Jerusalem (v. 26), where his Christian allegiance is made known by Barnabas to Jerusalem Christians, and his eventual departure for Caesarea, whence he was sent off to Tarsus (v. 30). In time, Barnabas seeks out Saul to bring him from Tarsus to Antioch, where they labor together "for a whole year" (11:25–26).

Eventually, Luke recounts the story of Saul's first missionary journey (Acts 13:1–14:28). He tells how Barnabas and Saul were set apart for this work on which the Spirit would send them, how they departed from Seleucia, the port of Antioch, and sailed for Cyprus, and how they evangelized the island. Sailing then from Paphos, they crossed to Perga in Pamphylia and passed on first to Antioch in Pisidia and further to towns of South Galatia, Iconium, Lystra, and Derbe, which they evangelized with some success. After mistreatment, however, they retraced their steps through Lystra, Iconium, and Antioch to return to Perga and sail from Attalia for Syrian Antioch. So runs the Lucan account of Paul's first missionary journey.

Since this part of the Lucan story of Paul's post-conversion years seems to have no correspondence in Paul's own letters, modern interpreters of Acts are sometimes skeptical about its historicity. In fact, Paul never recounts in narrative form these missionary movements, apart from a few verses of Galatians 1-2, which actually serve a rhetorical and apologetic purpose. In these chapters of Galatians, however, Paul tells how he returned to Damascus after his sojourn in Arabia (1:17c). Three years later he went up to Jerusalem for the first time after his conversion or call (1:18), *historēsai Kēphan,* "to seek information from Cephas" or "to visit Cephas." At the beginning of chapter 2 Paul writes, "Then during (the course of) fourteen years I went up again to Jerusalem with Barnabas, taking Titus along with me" (v. 1). I regard this visit as the so-called Council visit, the same as that recounted in Acts 15:1-12.

Yet in between the mention of these two visits to Jerusalem (1:18 and 2:1) Paul says explicitly that he went *eis ta klimata tēs Syrias kai tēs Kilikias,* "into the regions of Syria and Cilicia" (1:21). Paul insists that he was still personally unknown to the churches of Christ in Judea, which had "only heard that he who once persecuted us was now preaching the faith he had once tried to destroy" (1:23). He further specifies (2:2) that he had been "preaching among the Gentiles." Though it is difficult to state precisely what Paul might have meant by *klimata* (1:21), the word probably refers to "districts" or "subdivisions" within the Roman provinces of Syria and Cilicia.[7] There seems to be little doubt that the Lucan notice about Paul's withdrawal to Tarsus (Acts 9:30) can be correlated with "the region of Cilicia" (Gal 1:21). The fact that Mission I begins in Antioch on the Orontes (Acts 13:1-4) can also be correlated with the region of Syria (Gal 1:21). In any case, Paul insists that Christians in Judea had heard that he was "preaching the faith" (Gal 1:23), apparently in those "regions of Syria and Cilicia." The whole year of labor spent by Barnabas and Paul in Antioch is specified as "teaching a large number of people" (Acts 11:26). This may be the Lucan way of referring to what Paul meant by "preaching the faith" (Gal 1:23) to the Gentiles in the region of Syria in the period prior to the "Council."[8]

When Paul wrote to the Philippians, he mentioned "the beginning of the evangelization," in which he had been engaged (*en archē tou euangeliou,* 4:15). He recalled that, when he left Macedonia, no church entered into partnership with him in giving and receiving except the Philippian community; and he adds, "even in Thessalonica you sent me help once and again"

(4:16). Now "no church" could conceivably mean no other church in Macedonia (no one of which Paul ever mentions). But is it wholly out of question to maintain that Paul was thinking of "no other church" even in "the regions of Syria and Cilicia," where Gal 1:23 suggests that Paul did indeed begin his evangelization? It might even refer to churches in the areas evangelized by Paul in the pre-conciliar mission recounted in Acts 13:1–14:28. Paul must have passed to Philippi from the Province of Asia, where he may also have evangelized areas other than Syria and Cilicia. This last point is, of course, speculative, but the rest of the Lucan account of Mission I is not without some support in the sparse details about Paul's "preaching the faith" to Gentiles in the period before the so- *N B* called Council. Luke's account has supplied details that Paul has passed over for the sake of his rhetorical apology in Galatians. With this we may pass on to our third point.

### III. The Appearance of Paul
### before Gallio in Achaia

The correlation of the Pauline and Lucan data presented in part I above permits one to work out a relative chronology for Paul's missionary endeavors.[9] His appearance before the proconsul Gallio's tribunal in Achaia (Acts 18:12–17) supplies a date in Mission II that allows one to peg this incident in Paul's life absolutely, even though Paul himself never mentions it in his letters and only Luke records it. Though most interpreters of Paul's life and career acknowledge the historicity of this appearance before Gallio, there is still hesitation about the year in which it occurred. For this reason I should like to renew the discussion of it.

Lucius Annaeus Novatus was the son of M. Annaeus Seneca, a Roman *eques* and *rhetor,* and also the elder brother of the philosopher Seneca, the tutor of the emperor Nero. Lucius Junius Gallio was the name the former assumed when he was adopted by a wealthy friend and introduced to political life.

Gallio is mentioned as a friend of the emperor Claudius and as the proconsul of Achaia in a Greek inscription, which records the text of a letter sent by the emperor to the people of Delphi about a depopulation problem. Since the text itself is dated in the usual Roman fashion, one can establish by it the time when Gallio was proconsul in Achaia. The inscription had been set up in a temple of Apollo at Delphi, where it was discovered in fragmentary form in 1905 and 1910 by E. Bourguet.[10] The fragments, however, were not fully published until 1970 by A. Plassart.[11]

The main part of the Greek text of the inscription runs as follows:

1    *Tiber*[*ios Klaudios Kais*]*ar S*[*ebast*]*os G*[*ermanikos, dēmarchikēs exou*]

2    *sias* [*to IB, autokratōr t*]*o KZ, p*[*atēr p*]*atri*[*dos . . . . chairein*].

3    *Pal*[*ai men t*]*ēi p*[*olei tē*] *tōn Delph*[*ōn ēn o*]*u mo*[*non eunous all' epimelēs ty*]

4    *chēs aei d' etērē*[*sa tē*]*n thrēskei*[*an t*]*ou Apo*[*llōnos tou Pythiou· epei de*]

5    *nyn legetai kai* [*pol*]*eitōn erē*[*mo*]*s einai, hō*[*s moi arti apēngeile L. Iou*]

6    *nios Galliōn ho ph*[*ilos*] *mou ka*[*i anthy*]*patos,* [*boulomenos tous Delphous*]

7    *eti hexein ton pr*[*oteron kosmon entel*]*ē, e*[*tellomai hymein kai ex al*]

8    *lōn poleōn kal*[*ein eu gegonotas eis Delphous hōs neous katoikous kai*]

9    *autois epitre*[*pein ekgonois te ta*] *pres*[*beia panta echein ta tōn Del*]

10   *phōn hōs pole*[*itais ep' isē kai homoia. e*]*i men gar ti*[*nes . . . hōs polei*]

11   *tai metōkis*[*anto eis toutous tou*]*s topous, kr*[ . . . . . .]

[1]Tiber[ius Claudius Caes]ar A[ugust]us G[ermanicus, invested with tribunician po]wer [2][for the 12th time, acclaimed imperator for t]he 26th time, F[ather of the Fa]ther[land . . . sends greetings to . . .].[3] For a l[ong time I have been not onl]y [well disposed toward t]he ci[ty] of Delph[i, but also solicitous for its [4]pros]perity, and I have always sup[ported th]e cul[t of Pythian] Apol[lo. But] [5]now [since] it is said to be desti[tu]te of [citi]zens, as [L. Jun][6]ius Gallio, my fri[end] an[d procon]sul, [recently reported to me, and being

desirous that Delphi] [7]should continue to retain [inta]ct its for[mer rank, I] ord[er you (pl.) to in]vite [well-born people also from [8]ot]her cities [to Delphi as new inhabitants and to] [9]all[ow] them [and their children to have all the] privi[leges of Del]phi [10]as being citi[zens on equal and like (basis)]. For i[f] so[me . . . [11]were to trans[fer as citi]zens [to those regions. . . .[12]

From the text of the letter one may deduce that Gallio was proconsul of Achaia during the twelfth regnal year of the emperor Claudius (A.D. 41–54) and after the twenty-sixth acclamation of him as imperator. The emperor was invested with *potestas tribunicia* each year, and that investment marked his regnal years. The emperor's name and the twelfth year of this tribunician authority has in large part been restored in this inscription, but the restorations are certain because of other known inscriptions of Claudius.[13] His twelfth regnal year began on 25 January A.D. 52. The acclamation of him as *imperator* was sporadic, since it usually depended on military victories in which he would have been engaged or at least indirectly involved. To date an event by such acclamations one has to learn when such and such an acclamation occurred. From other inscriptions one knows that the twenty-second to the twenty-fifth acclamations took place in Claudius' eleventh regnal year (25 January A.D. 51 to 24 January A.D. 52) and that the twenty-seventh acclamation occurred in his twelfth regnal year, before 1 August A.D. 52. Theoretically, then, the twenty-sixth acclamation could have occurred before the winter of A.D. 51 or in the spring of A.D. 52. The matter is settled, however, by an inscription that has often been neglected in the recent discussion of Pauline chronology in the light of this Delphi inscription mentioning Gallio. A Greek inscription from Kys in Caria, published in 1887, combines the twenty-sixth acclamation with the twelfth regnal year: *dēmarchikēs exousias to dōdekaton, hypaton to penpton, autokratora to eikoston kai hekton,* "with tribunician authority for the twelfth time, consul for the fifth, imperator for the twenty-sixth time."[14] From this it is now clear that the combination of the twelfth regnal year of Claudius with the twenty-sixth acclamation of him as *imperator* points to a time between 25 January and 1 August A.D. 52. Claudius would have written the letter to the people of Delphi sometime in this period, and in it he refers to L. Junius Gallio as his friend and proconsul of Achaia.

Since Achaia was a senatorial province of praetorian rank, it was governed by a proconsul (Greek *anthypatos;* cf. Acts 18:12; 13:7; Josephus, *Ant.* 14.10.21 §244). Such a provincial governor was in office for a year and was expected to assume his post by 1 June,[15] and to leave for the province by mid-April at the latest.[16] Claudius's letter mentions that Gallio has reported to him about the conditions he found in Delphi on his arrival. This would seem to mean that Gallio was already in Achaia by late spring or early summer of A.D. 52 and had written to the emperor Claudius about them.

The problem has always been to decide whether Gallio's proconsular year in Achaia stretched from sometime in A.D. 51–52 or from sometime in A.D. 52–53.[17] Since Seneca, Gallio's younger brother, reports that Gallio developed a fever in Achaia and "took ship immediately,"[18] it seems that Gallio cut short his proconsular stay in Achaia and hurried back home. This suggests that Gallio arrived in Achaia in the late spring of A.D. 52, reported on conditions to the emperor Claudius, spent the summer there, and departed from the province not later than the end of October A.D. 52, before *mare clausum,* when ship-travel on the Mediterranean became impossible because of the danger of winter storms. It follows then that Paul would have been haled before Gallio in the late spring, summer, or early fall of A.D. 52.[19]

If one accepts the Lucan testimony that Paul's stay in Corinth toward the end of Mission II lasted for eighteen months (Acts 18:11),[20] then Paul would have arrived in Corinth in the early part of the year A.D. 51.

These, then, are the aspects of the Lucan story of Paul's missionary journeys that merit our reconsideration. On the basis of such considerations one can further work out the chronology of Paul's life and missionary journeys.[21] The proper understanding of what we can learn about the life and missionary movements of Paul helps in the comprehension of his epistolary heritage. For his writings did not drop from a vacuum; they were all related to real-life situations and problems with which he coped. The attempt, then, to work out the chronology of the Apostle's ministry enables us to situate his writings properly.

# CHAPTER FOUR

# Abba *and Jesus'* *Relation to God*

It is well known that in the New Testament Jesus is depicted praying to God during his agony in the garden and addressing him as *abba* (Mark 14:36). Paul too is aware of this mode of addressing God when he speaks of the Spirit-inspired prayer of Christians in Gal 4:6 and Rom 8:15. Paul understands it as a sign of the adoptive sonship enjoyed by Christians because of the Spirit of Jesus that they have received. The implication is that they too, like Jesus of Nazareth, can call upon God, addressing him as *abba*. This is a feature that is important to Pauline christology.

In each case, the Greek translation, *ho patēr,* has been added, and its addition became the beginning of a centuries-old debate about whether the historical Jesus of Nazareth could have used such a mode of address, what its connotations might have been, what its relation might be to other uses of "Father" found on the lips of Jesus in the Gospels, and finally what implications it has for the study of New Testament christology. Indeed, apart from the prayer of praise addressed by Jesus to the Father in the Synoptics (Luke 10:21–22; Matt 11:25–27), it is perhaps the closest thing we have in these Gospels that would give an inkling of Jesus' own awareness of his relationship to God.

The so-called *abba*-problem has been the subject of no little recent debate because of the research of Joachim Jeremias and reactions to it.[1] There are philological aspects of the problem

47

as well as historical and christological, and they all have to be reckoned with, for each one of them affects the problem as a whole. As in every debate, there has been the tendency either to make the evidence say too little or too much, and so there is reason to survey the data that we have at disposal at present to see whether a course can be steered between Scylla and Charybdis and what can be salvaged from the critical approaches that have been taken toward this problem. I propose then to devote attention to (I) the philological aspects of the *abba*-problem, (II) its historical aspects, and (III) its christological aspects.

## I. The Philological Aspects of the *Abba*-Problem

When Origen, who otherwise knew well his Greek and Semitic languages, commented on *abba,* he regarded the word, strangely enough, as a "Hebrew term" (*hē hebraikē lexis*).[2] It remained for Jerome, however, to straighten out the explanation: "It is Syrian, not Hebrew" (*syrum est, non hebraeum*).[3] In using *syrum,* Jerome was employing the name current in his day for what we would more accurately call today Aramaic, for Greek *abba* is the transcription of Aramaic *'abbā'*.

Aramaic *'abbā'* is often explained as a child's word, a baby's babbling sound with a special familiar connotation, much like English "papa" or "daddy."[4] The doubling of the *b* in the form may well bear witness to such an origin, since it is a form of *'ab,* "father" (from Protosemitic *'abu*) and may have been influenced by its female counterpart *'immā',* "mother," where the doubling of *m* is original (from Protosemitic *'immu*). I shall return to this aspect below.

Aramaic *'abbā'* has been regarded as the emphatic state of the noun *'ab,* meaning "the father."[5] One would normally expect the emphatic state to be *'ăbā'* or possibly *'ăbāh,* with a reduced vowel in the pretonic syllable, as it is in some other forms of Aramaic.[6] The Greek *abba,* however, with the doubled *beta* clearly reflects the Aramaic form *'abbā'* that is attested in vocalized texts from antiquity.

However, since the end of the last century scholars such as
T. Nöldeke, E. Littmann, G. Kittel, J. Barr, and more recently
Jeremias,[7] have tried to maintain the form *'abbā'* is not the
emphatic state of *'ab* but a special form developed by the
addition of an (originally Protosemitic) adverbial ending *-ā'*
to become a vocative. Though this explanation may sound
plausible, it must be remembered that that would be a unique
vocative in a Semitic language that otherwise lacks a special
vocative form and that normally uses the emphatic state precisely to express the vocative. Thus, *malkā' lĕʿālĕmîn hĕyî,* "O
King, live forever!" (Dan 2:4).[8] There is no reason, then, to
invoke the survival of an ancient ending *-ā'* to explain what
otherwise appears to be an emphatic state. As G. Schelbert has
recently remarked in this regard: "In such a hypothesis [that
the form is a vestige of a protosemitic vocative] it seems problematic indeed that *'abbā'* has not left the slightest trace in all
of Hebrew literature — or in Aramaic literature — prior to the
first century A.D. That is quite unlikely for such a 'homely word'
[*sic*], if this assumption were exact."[9] Finally, the doubling of
the *b* in this emphatic state is clearly secondary (see the preceding paragraph) and can be paralleled in other words in
Aramaic, when an effort was made to preserve a full short vowel
in a pretonic syllable.[10]

The Greek translation added to *'abbā'* obviously regarded
the form as an emphatic state, since it used *ho patēr*. This literal
translation has been said to be "not correct Greek usage,"[11]
since the Greek language has a vocative for addressing a person and could have rendered *'abbā'* properly as *páter,* the very
form used in Luke 22:42, where the evangelist avoids the foreign
word because of his predominantly Gentile Greek-speaking
readers.

However, in both classical and hellenistic Greek the nominative case, with and without the article, was used at times
as a substitute for the vocative. Thus in Homer, *dēmoboros
basileus,* "O folk-devouring king!" (*Iliad* 1. 231); in Xenophon,
*hymeis hoi hēgemones . . . pros eme pantes symballete . . . ,*
"You, O officers, all of you gather to me. . . !" (*Cyrop.* 6.2.41).
Moreover, the nominative of simple words was especially used
for servants and inferiors: *ho pais,* "Boy!" instead of the

vocative *pai* (Aristophanes, *Frogs* 521; cf. *Acharn*. 243; *Birds* 665–66).[12] In the LXX, instead of *theé,* "O God," the nominative *ho theos* was often used (e.g. Ps 5:11; 36:8; 44:2; 54:3); and in the New Testament such a nominative is further found (Mark 9:25; Luke 8:54; 10:21e; 11:39; 18:11,13; Matt 11:26; John 13:13; 19:3; Eph 5:14; 6:1; Rev 4:11; 6:10; 12:12; 15:3; 16:5; 18:4,20; 19:5).[13] Moreover, Aramaic *ṭalyĕtā'*/*ṭalyĕtā'* is written in Greek as *talitha* and translated with the Greek articular nominative *to korasion,* "O maiden" (Mark 5:41). So when the Greek translation was added to *abba* (the vestige of a Palestinian Aramaic form) the articular nominative not only reflected the emphatic state of the original but also made use of a not-too-common, but certainly correct Greek usage to do so.

## II. The Historical Aspects
## of the *Abba*-Problem

When one looks for evidence of the form *'abbā'*[14] in early Aramaic, one is struck by its absence, at least as a common noun. There is no occurrence of the emphatic state of this noun in Old Aramaic (ca. 925–700 B.C.).[15] Moreover, in the Imperial or Official phase of the language (700–200 B.C.), it appears sporadically as a proper name, Abba,[16] or as a patronymic *bar 'Abbā'* or *bar 'Abbāh*.[17] It is only in the Middle phase of the language (roughly 200 B.C.–A.D. 200) that it begins to appear with some regularity, both as a proper name or a patronymic and as a common noun. Various forms of the noun *'ab* are, to be sure, attested in the Old and Imperial phases of the language, among which *'by* (= *'ăbî,* "my father") is found frequently enough.[18] That form is even found in Dan 5:13 and is the one that *'abbā'* is said to replace in time.

In the period of Middle Aramaic, in which we are interested because Aramaic as the language that Jesus would most frequently have spoken belongs to this phase of it, the following forms of *'ab* should be noted:

*'ab* (absolute state), "a father": 11QtgJob 31:5 (= Hebrew Job 38:28).[19]

'*ăbî*, "my father": 1QapGen 2:19;[20] 1QTLevi ar (= 1Q21)
29;[21] 4QTLevi ar[a] 2:12;[22] 4QEn[c] 5 ii 17;[23] 4QTQahat frg.
1:11;[24] 6QEnGiants (= 6Q8) 1:4;[25] pap5/6HevA nab
1:6,7; 3:1.[26]

'*ăbî*, "O my father" (vocative): 1QapGen 2,24 (*yā*' '*ăbî wĕyā*'
*mārî*, "O my father and my lord").[27]

'*ăbûnāh*, "our father": Jerusalem Hypogeum Ossuary 1b.[28]

'*Abbāh*, "Abba" (proper name): Giv'at HaMivtar Tomb
Inscription;[29] possibly also in the Trilingual Jerusalem
Ossuary (if the text is to be translated, "Abba buried his
son").[30]

'*abbā*', "Abba" (as a title): Jerusalem Hypogeum Ossuary
1a;[31] Mur 87;[32] Silwan Tomb Ossuary 2.[33]

The upshot of the foregoing presentation is that one still finds
for the address "O my father" the form '*ăbî* in these Aramaic
texts. When '*abbā*'/'*abbāh* does occasionally occur in them,
it is as either a proper name or a patronymic or a title or possibly
the formal usage, "Father." In no instance has it certainly
replaced '*ăbî* or been found as a child's word, since it is used
by adults who inscribe funerary texts with it in one of the senses
mentioned. It is never used of God.

When the Mishnah was finally codified and set to writing
under Rabbi Judah the Prince toward the beginning of the third
century A.D., Aramaic '*abbā*' was introduced into its Hebrew
text.[34] Here too the meaning of '*abbā*' varies: (a) Sometimes
it serves as an honorific title for a sage or rabbi: Abba Saul,
Abba Jose, Abba Eleazar;[35] (b) in one passage it seems to be
a personal name, Abba;[36] (c) in another it is used as an address,
"Father" (*m. 'Ed.* 5:7); but (d) it frequently stands in passages
where it is parallel to or is used in connection with possessive
forms like "my father." Thus in a contrast, '*abbā*' *gādôl
mē'ăbîkā* (*m. Sanh.* 4:5), which H. Danby translates, "My
father was greater than thy father."[37] Indeed, the possessive
sense of Hebrew '*ābî* is completely replaced by '*abbā*' in the
Mishnah, and the form '*ābî* occurs only as the Hebrew construct state. This usage has made some scholars translate
Mishnaic '*abbā*' always "my father."[38] But (e) it may be queried
whether that meaning is always present, since in some Mishnaic
passages it seems to mean little more than the formal "Father."[39]

In the Mishnah, *'abbā'* is never used of God, not even in *m. Sotah* 9:15, where it might have been expected: "On whom can we depend? Only on our Father in heaven" (*'al 'ābînû šebbaššāmayîm*).

What one finds, then, in the Mishnaic usage is confirmed in the classic targums of Onqelos (of the Pentateuch) and Jonathan (of the Prophets) in the rabbinic period.[40] In appealing to such Aramaic texts, one has to reckon with them as examples of Late Aramaic, i.e. the form of the language that came into existence about A.D. 200.[41] What is found in these texts that may seem to bear on the *abba*-problem is not necessarily characteristic of Palestinian Aramaic of the first century A.D.

Many forms of Hebrew *'āb* occur in the Pentateuch and the Prophets, but fortunately most of them have little bearing on the *abba*-problem and can be neglected. What is of importance for this discussion is the way(s) in which certain forms of the word are translated into Aramaic in the earlier of the classic targums. These forms are the absolute *'āb,* "father," and the possessive *'ābî,* "my father."[42]

*hā'āb* (article + absolute), "the father," translated as *'abbā':* Ezek 18:4,19.

*'āb* (absolute), "(a) father," translated as *'abbā'.*[43] Note that Aramaic absolute *'ab* is correctly used in Mal 1:6b. It is also so used in Num 11:12 to translate Hebrew *hārîtî,* "Have I conceived?" which becomes *hǎ'ab lě-,* "Have I become a father to . . . ?"; cf. Gen 44:19,20; 45:8; Josh 22:14; Ezek 18:20; 22:7,10; Mic 7:6; Mal 1:6a; 2:10 (said of God).[44]

*'ābî* (in statements), "my father," translated as *'abbā':* Gen 19:34; 20:12,13; 31:42; Josh 2:12,13; Judg 6:15.

*'ābî* (in addresses), "O my father," translated as *'abbā':* Gen 22:7; 27:18,34,38; 48:18; Judg 11:36; Isa 8:4.[45]

What one notices in this targumic material is the widespread use of *'abbā',* and in one instance even for God (Mal 2:10), in a statement, but not in an address. That such a development should have taken place is not surprising, and the use of *'abbā'* continues to develop.[46]

To understand, however, the import of the historical data presented above, one has to recall the background of the Old Testament material which bears on the *abba*-problem, for God is referred to in the Old Testament as Father. Not only is Israel described as his children or his firstborn (e.g. Exod 4:22–23; Deut 14:1; Isa 30:9; Hos 11:1–3), but the title is used explicitly of God, when he is considered as creator (Deut 32:6; Mal 2:10), as lord of his chosen people, who is to be obeyed (Jer 3:19; 31:9; Isa 63:16), as the one sinned against by Israel (Jer 3:4–5; Mal 1:16), and as the one from whom come assistance, mercy, and forgiveness (Ps 103:13; Isa 64:7–8). God is acknowledged by Israel as "our Father" (Isa 63:16; 64:8), and David or the king addresses God as "my Father" (Ps 89:27). Yet in all these passages God is so viewed in his capacity as Father of corporate or national Israel.[47]

The use of "Father" by an individual Palestinian Jew in addressing God is rare in the Old Testament. It may be attested in deuterocanonical Sir 23:1,4: "O Lord, Father and Ruler/God of my life." But that address is found only in the Greek text of Sirach, is not extant in the Hebrew, and has been paraphrased differently in a later Hebrew liturgical text which depends on it: "Say to the one who fashioned you, 'God of my father and Lord of my life.'"[48]

Again, at first sight an instance of such usage seems to occur in one of the Thanksgiving Psalms from Qumran, which uses Hebrew *'āb* of God: "For you are father to all [the sons of] your truth; and you rejoice over them as one who has conceived over her child" (1QH 9:35–36), which is possibly an echo of Prov 23:25. But in this text God is acknowledged as father in a corporate sense, as the father of the community.[49] However, the vocative use of Hebrew *'ābî* has recently turned up in two Qumran texts: *'ābî wē'lōhay, 'al ta'azbēnî bēyad haggōyîm,* "my Father and my God, abandon me not into the hands of the Gentiles" (4Q372 1:16); and *'ābî wa'ădōnî,* "my Father and my Lord" (4Q460 5:6).[50] In these cases, we have for the first time clear examples of an individual Jew addressing God as "my Father" in pre-Christian Palestinian Hebrew texts. Yet it is still not the same as the Aramaic *'abbā'.*

In all his research into the matter J. Jeremias was able to point to only two instances in the writing of pre-Christian

Palestinian Judaism in which the title appears, and these are in deuterocanonical books: Tob 13:4, "because he is the Lord our God, our Father and God forever," again in a corporate sense; and Sir 51:10, "I extolled the Lord, 'You are my Father,'" usually judged to be an echo of David's prayer mentioned above; even if this were considered valid, it would still be a statement, not an address or a vocative.[51]

Jeremias himself claimed to have found two instances in which *'abbā'* was used in pre-Christian Palestinian Jewish writing, instances that he regarded as crucial in his view of the development by which *'abbā'* took over from *'ăbî* and came "to an end in the New Testament Period."[52] The first tells of Šim'on ben Šeṭaḥ, who rebukes Ḥoni for acting petulantly before God, as a son before his father: "'Father, take me to bathe in warm water, wash me in cold water, give me nuts, almonds, peaches, and pomegranates'; and he gives them to him." Here *'abbā'* is used indirectly of God in a Hebrew text.[53] In another passage, school children are sent to Ḥoni to cry, "'Father, Father, give us rain.' Thereupon he would plead with the Holy One, Blessed be He, [thus]: 'Master of the Universe, do it for the sake of these who are unable to distinguish between the Father who gives rain and the father who does not.'" Here *'abbā'* is used of the one who gives rain.[54] But both these texts are drawn from the fifth-century *Babylonian* Talmud and cannot without further ado be taken as evidence for first-century Palestinian Jewish usage. G. Schelbert has recently subjected them to minute analysis and comes out against Jeremias's unwarranted use of them.[55]

Jeremias is correct in complaining against undocumented assertions about *'abbā'* as a common designation for God in the Palestinian Judaism of Jesus' time, especially when the use of the title without modifiers (such as "in heaven," "my," "our," etc.) is considered.[56] Again, Jeremias may be right when he detects a development in Judaism "with the emergence of a new vocabulary."[57] He ascribes to Yoḥanan ben Zakkai, "a contemporary of the apostles," the influence that led to the introduction of the phrase, "our heavenly Father," into theological (i.e. rabbinical) language. Yet the sources of Jeremias's information for this development are the Tannaitic midrashim, which are at the earliest of late second-century or early third-century provenience and cannot be facilely equated with the period of Yoḥanan ben Zakkai himself (A.D. 50–80). Moreover, even if this title "heavenly Father" were attested in first-century Palestinian Judaism and were to serve as the background for the Matthean usage, which is not unlikely, it still has little to say about the use of *'abbā'* alone.

Given this historical situation about the use of *'ab, 'ăbî,* and *'abbā'* in pre-Christian Palestinian Aramaic usage, in the Hebrew of the Mishnah, and in the classic targums, it is not surprising that *'abbā'* is eventually extended to God himself, especially in light of the Old Testament material that is also part of the background of the usage. What is noteworthy is the length of time that one has to wait to see *'abbā'* emerge as a common noun, as a title, and as an address. Jeremias was still tied to a rabbinic mode of formulating his emphatic statement — *"there is as yet no evidence in the literature of ancient Palestinian Judaism that 'my Father' is used as a personal address to God"*[58] — his statement now needs to be corrected in light of the two Qumran examples cited above. Similarly, when he writes, "For Jesus to address God as 'my Father' is therefore something new,"[59] he is no longer right. It would be better formulated, however, thus: There is no evidence in the literature of pre-Christian or first-century Palestinian Judaism that *'abbā'* was used in any sense as a personal address for God by an individual Jew — and for Jesus to address God as *'abbā'* or "Father" is therefore something new.

The earliest attestation of such usage remains that given by Paul in an otherwise Greek letter (Gal 4:6), written in the mid-fifties of the first century, and it may be an echo of a tradition about a prayer uttered by Jesus himself, later recorded in Mark 14:36. This actually brings my discussion to the threshold of the christological aspects of the *abba*-problem, but there are still other historical aspects of the problem that need comment.

Writers who have been impressed by Jeremias's research have often concluded similarly. F. Hahn has written that *abba* is to "be regarded with certainty as a mark of Jesus' manner of speech," since it is otherwise "unthinkable in the prayer language of contemporary Judaism."[60] W. G. Kümmel acknowledges that this identification of God as Father by Jesus has been recognized as "striking and unusual" in the Judaism of his day, even "quite extraordinary."[61]

However, G. Vermes queries whether such "positive and summary assertions take sufficient notice of the facts of Jewish history."[62] He claims rather that "one of the distinguishing features of ancient Hasidic piety" was "its habit of alluding to God precisely as 'Father,'" and in support of his claim he quotes the following as part of *m. Ber.* 5:1: "The ancient Hasidim spent an hour (in recollection before praying) in order to direct their hearts towards their Father in heaven."[63] When, however, one glances at the Hebrew text of this Mishnaic passage, one finds the following: *Ḥăsîdîm hārî'šōnîm hāyû šōhîm šā'āh 'aḥat ûmitpallĕlîm kĕdê šeyyĕkawwĕnû 'et libbām lammāqôm.*[64] Literally translated, this sentence means: "The first Hasidim used to spend one hour and pray in order to direct their heart to the Place." H. Danby translates the passage as follows: "The pious old men of old used to wait an hour before they said the *Tefillah,* that they might direct their heart toward God."[65] Here the Mishnah is undoubtedly using the surrogate for "God" that is found in Esth 4:14 (*māqôm*).[66]

In the Giessen edition of the Mishnah,[67] however, one does find instead of *lammāqôm* the clause *la'ăbîhem šebbaššāmāyim,* "to their Father who is in heaven." This, of course, immediately raises the question, Which is the more primitive form of the Mishnah statement? Since the latter form is also found in *m. Ber.* 5:1 as cited in the Babylonian Talmud (*b. Ber.* 30b),[68] this suggests that it is not the more primitive form. In any case, Vermes should have called attention to this variant in some editions of the Mishnah, for it considerably undercuts the argument that he tries to build on this passage. It should also be noted that the form is *'ăbîhem,* "their father," and not *'abbā',* i.e. that it is suffixal and not the Aramaic form, which is the point at issue. Further, the added relative clause, "who is in heaven," again raises the question about "the emergence of a new vocabulary," a phrase cited from Jeremias.[69] Hence one may wonder whether "the facts of Jewish history," as marshalled by Vermes, really have any value in the discussion of historical aspects of the *abba*-problem.[70]

So far we have seen that the Greek *abba* of the New

Testament remains the earliest attestation of this term in a vocative sense. Its occurrence in Gal 4:6 and Rom 8:15 bears witness to its use as a form of address for God in the fifties, and that in Mark 14:36 to its use ca. A.D. 65. No one will contest a claim that it is undoubtedly rooted in earlier Palestinian custom, but how much earlier remains problematic.

Yet since it is always fitted with a Greek translation, *ho patēr,* in the New Testament, another aspect of the historical problem must be considered. Aramaic or Hebrew words are sometimes used in the Greek New Testament without a translation (e.g. *maranatha, hōsanna, allēlouia, amēn*), but others are translated (e.g. *talitha* and *to korasion, messias* and *christos, rabbi* and *didaskale*). The translation has been added to make the Aramaic or Hebrew expression clear to Greek-speaking Gentile Christians. But it also raises the question whether the addition of such a translation betrays a community matrix for the formula. Does the Pauline use of the formula *abba ho patēr* in Spirit-inspired community prayer point to such an origin? E. Haenchen is undoubtedly right in contending that Jesus himself would never have used Aramaic *'abbā'* along with the following Greek translation and that the combination was "a formula in use in a Hellenistic community."[71] He further contends that Mark put this form of address for God, which was customary in such a community, on the lips of Jesus in 14:36, indeed in depicting a scene in which there were no witnesses listening. Haenchen is careful to admit that this does not mean that Jesus never addressed God "with the Aramaic word *'abbā',*" and he is right to insist that Jesus in prayer is not presented in the Synoptics as always making use of *'abbā'* (apart from Mark 15:34).[72]

Yet another aspect of the problem remains. Why would *'abbā'* have been retained in Greek-speaking communities? Luke 22:42 and John 17:1,5,11,25 show that the good Greek vocative *páter* was being used to address God in some Greek-speaking communities. There is sufficient other testimony in both the Synoptic and Johannine traditions to reveal that Jesus' relationship to God was expressed in terms of Father and Son.[73] This then would support Jeremias's contention that *'abbā'* was indeed *ipsissima vox Jesu*. It was preserved in his own mother-tongue, even in Greek-speaking communities, precisely as a recollection and a sign of his use of it. It was scarcely preserved as *onoma thespesion ē rhēsis barbarikē*, "a holy name or foreign phrase," as Lucian (*Philopseudes* 9) liked to caricature the use of foreign words in miracle-stories, since '*abbā*' never occurs in such a story. The preservation of the Aramaic word is thus a strong argument for the recollection of a term used by the Jesus of history.

### III. The Christological Aspects of the *Abba*-Problem

There is no need to present in detail Jesus' use of "Father" for God, since this has already been adequately done by Jeremias.[74] I shall summarize here briefly his salient conclusions in order to press on further. *First,* Jeremias called attention to the frequency of the designation "Father" in the Gospels, 170 times in all; and to the diversity and distribution of it in that tradition: 4 instances in Mark, 15 in Luke, 42 in Matthew, and 109 in John. If one isolates the instances when Jesus is depicted addressing God as Father in prayer, then there are 3 instances in Mark, 4 in "Q," 4 in "L," 3 in "M," and 100 in John. From such data Jeremias concludes to "*a growing tendency to introduce the title 'Father' for God into the sayings of Jesus.*"[75] Jeremias ascribes this tendency to "Christian prophets" in the early communities who spoke in the name of the exalted Lord and with his words. That tendency came to its logical conclusion in the Johannine Gospel.

*Second,* when the designation "Father" (without personal pronouns) is considered, Mark has only one instance of it (13:32), "Q" has none, "L" has two (Luke 9:26; 11:13), and "M" has one (Matt 28:19), whereas John has 73 instances. Of these only Mark 13:32 and Luke 11:13 are considered by Jeremias as serious contenders for the authentic usage of Jesus himself.[76] Jeremias further treats of "your Father" in "Jesus' didache to his disciples," but that does not really concern us here. Of more importance is the use of "my Father," which also has a varied distribution; it occurs perhaps once in Mark 8:38,[77] once in "Q" (Luke 10:22 = Matt 11:27), three times in "L" (Luke 2:49; 22:29; 24:49), 13 times in "M," and 25 times

in John. Of these passages Jeremias would consider only four
as authentic: Mark 13:32; Matt 11:27 = Luke 10:22; Matt
16:17; Luke 22:29. All of these have to do with "the specific
relationship of Jesus to God," the basis of his revelation and
authority.

*Third,* the foregoing data provide the background for judging
the most crucial passages in the New Testament in which Jesus
addresses God as "Father":

> In "Mk": *abba* (Mark 14:36), which Luke 22:42 renders
> simply as *páter* and for which Matt 26:39 substitutes *páter
> mou;* the last form is to be regarded as a translation not
> of Aramaic *'abbā',* but of Aramaic *'ăbî,* which was in con-
> temporary use.[78]
>
> In "Q": *páter* (Luke 11:2), for which Matt 6:9 substitutes
> rather *páter hēmōn ho en tois ouranois.*[79] *Páter* and *ho
> patēr* are both vocative (Luke 10:21ab = Matt 11:25,26).
>
> In "L": *páter* (Luke 23:46).[80]
>
> In John: *páter* (11:41; 12:27,28; 17:1,5,11,25, etc.).

Of these instances Jeremias would trace to Stage I of the
gospel tradition[81] the *páter* of the Lucan "Our Father" (11:2),
Jesus' praise of the Father (Luke 10:21 = 11:25,26), and the
Gethsemane prayer with *'abbā'* (Mark 14:36).

When we recognize the full-blown tradition in Stage III, there
is little doubt that much of the data in it comes from Stage
II (in which Jeremias found the "growing tendency" to introduce
the title). Yet a cautious look at all aspects of the *abba*-problem
seems to call for the recognition that some part of the tradition was rooted in an attitude of Jesus himself in his historical
ministry, i.e. it does not all stem from Stage II.

That, however, leaves open the question about the sense in
which *'abbā'* would have been used by Jesus of Nazareth. E.
Haenchen[82] claims that when Rabbi Sadoq ca. A.D. 70 —
Haenchen acknowledges that this is found in a tradition of late
vintage[83] — entered the (destroyed) Jerusalem Temple and
prayed, "My Father, who are in heaven," or when one recited
the *Šĕmōnēh 'Eśrēh* and said, "Forgive us, Our Father," there
was no basic difference in language from Jesus' usage that is
discernible. On the surface this may seem true, but this is to

ride roughshod over distinctions that have been drawn earlier in this paper, such as the corporate or national sense of "Father" in contrast with that of an individual or the "emergence of new vocabulary" not current in the time of Jesus himself. Part of the problem here is that the New Testament tradition attributes not just "Father" (*páter*) or "my Father" (*páter mou*) to Jesus, but even *'abbā'*, which, as we have seen, stands a good chance of being *ipsissima vox Jesu*. Haenchen is supposed to be commenting on Mark 14:36, but he obfuscates the issue with his consideration of other, pronominal forms of address.

Jeremias concluded from his study of the Jewish and New Testament evidence that "'my Father' on the lips of Jesus expresses a unique relationship with God."[84] He based the conclusion mainly on his evidence that in all of pre-Christian Palestinian literature there is no instance of God being addressed as *'abbā'* by an individual Jew in prayer. "For Jesus to venture to take this step was something new and unheard of."[85] It is the claim of the *uniqueness* of the relationship that causes the problem for some commentators.[86] That is a conclusion that is drawn from what is admittedly negative evidence, since one would normally expect that, since *abba* is found in New Testament Greek, it would be attested in pre-Christian Jewish writings, if it is to be traced back to Jesus, a Palestinian Jew. But the fact is that this address for God is unattested in such pre-Christian sources, and the claim that Jesus' use of it is "new and unheard of" is not wholly unlikely. Part of the problem here is that which is associated with *all* the Jesus-tradition in the New Testament; it comes to us filtered through Stages II and III of the gospel tradition, and any attempt to reach a certain conclusion about Stage I is fraught with difficulty.

Part of the problem too is Jeremias' association of the "unique relationship" with "the chatter of a small child": "He spoke to God like a child to its father, simply, inwardly, confidently. Jesus' use of *abba* in addressing God reveals the heart of his relationship with God."[87] True, Jeremias did subsequently state that one could not assume that Jesus actually spoke to his heavenly Father like a small child, "a piece of inadmissible naivety." Indeed, his evidence showed that adults and grown-up sons so addressed their fathers; and E. Haenchen rightly recognized that Jeremias himself had "destroyed" the force of such an argument.[88] The origin of the form *'abbā'* as a baby-word might have to be admitted (see p. 48 above); but it scarcely bears on the address as a formulation of a "unique" relationship. In other words, if *'abbā'* is an expression of a unique filiation on Jesus' lips, it does not come merely from the use of such a baby-term and has to be shown in another way.

I have stated my reasons above for regarding *'abbā'* as *ipsissima vox Jesu,* as an Aramaic address used by him to express his relationship to God. If uniqueness is to be attributed to that relationship, however, one finds it expressed not in *'abbā'* alone, but also in Jesus' prayer of praise preserved in Luke 10:21–22 and Matt 11:25–27, which has been derived by the evangelists from "Q." It is cited here in the Lucan form:

> [21]I praise you, Father, Lord of heaven and earth, because you have hidden these things from the wise and intelligent, yet have revealed them to small children. Indeed, Father, this has been your good pleasure.
> [22]All things have been entrusted to me by my Father. No one knows who the Son is but the Father, or who the Father is but the Son, or the one to whom the Son chooses to reveal him.

I am more interested in the revelatory utterance in v. 22 than in the praise of the Father in v. 21. I am aware of the debate whether vv. 21-22 were originally a unit, an issue to which J. Dupont once addressed himself,[89] and whether its origin is to be sought in a Hellenistic or Egyptian background or rather in a Jewish or Old Testament setting.[90] Such questions do not concern us now.

In the Lucan form of this prayer it is Spirit-inspired, and Jesus recognizes the Father to whom he prays as the Lord or Sovereign of heaven and earth, of that realm from which Satan has been seen falling (10:18) and in which his disciples' names have been inscribed (10:20). But this Father is also lord of the realm in which Jesus' own ministry and teaching have been manifested. He extols this Lord and Father who has seen fit to reveal eschatological secrets, not to the wise and intelligent of this world, but to his chosen disciples, the "small children," the *in-fantes* who stand in the tradition of the genuine recipients of Israel's wisdom of old. What they have seen and heard has been a revelation from the Father himself. It has come to the disciples because it is a manifestation of the Father's "good pleasure" (10:21; recall 2:14). Verse 22 explains the revelation: not only the relation of Jesus to this heavenly Father, but also the relation the disciples to him. He alone reveals all these things, and precisely as "the Son." If the sense of *tauta*, "these things" (10:21) in its original setting (Stage I) escapes us, it refers in this Lucan context (Stage III) to the hidden meaning of what the disciples have seen and heard in Jesus' ministry and teaching in Galilean towns. Again, if the sense of the original *panta*, "all things" (10:22) escapes us, it refers in the Lucan (and Matthean) context to the knowledge that the Son has about the Father and the knowledge that only he can transmit to his followers, the "little children." Verse 22c expresses the sheer gratuity of this definitive revelation now being made known to human beings. Herein lies the uniqueness of the relationship of the Son to the Father, of Jesus to God. As a result, the later Christian tradition of the first century would eventually develop so that Jesus would be acknowledged not only as "Son of God," but even as "God" (John 1:1; 20:28; Heb 1:8).[91] But it should be stressed that, even if he is eventually called *theos*, he is such as *ho huios*, "the Son" (1 Cor 15:28; Mark 13:32); he is not himself *'abbā'* or *ho patēr*.

Can this prayer of praise really be traced back to Jesus of Nazareth in Stage I of the gospel tradition? There is probably no more disputed saying in that tradition than this one, when the question of authenticity is raised. E. Norden, A. von Harnack, M. Dibelius, R. Bultmann, E. Klostermann, J. M. Creed, W. G. Kümmel, G. Bornkamm, C. K. Barrett, M. J. Suggs[92] have either queried or denied its authenticity. But it has not gone without its defenders: G. Dalman, J. Chapman, R. Otto, W. Manson, T. W. Manson, J. Schmid, J. Schniewind, A. M. Hunter, and A. Feuillet.[93] Even when one considers the parallels to the sayings in Luke 10:21–22 in ancient extrabiblical literature or in the Johannine tradition and makes allowance for obvious redactional modifications of the evangelists, it is difficult to be apodictic and deny to Jesus himself the revelatory contents of these verses. For he must have said or insinuated something similar to what is recorded here to give rise to the rapid conclusion that surfaced not long after his death, that he was indeed the Son of God (even if that were not yet understood with the full nuances of the Council of Nicaea). Though I am inclined to regard the substance of these sayings as authentic, that substance may have to be traced only to an implicit formulation in Jesus' own words and deeds. But that substance would include some inkling of the uniqueness of the relationship between him and the Father as *'abbā'*, whom he actually so addressed.

Finally, if there is any validity in this way of discussing the philological, historical, and christological aspects of the *abba*-problem, it might make its own not-unimportant contribution to the study of New Testament christology, and especially to Pauline christology. For it is to the Apostle of the Gentiles that we are indebted for the earliest trace of the tradition that uses of Christians a formula that Jesus used himself. It not only tells us how Paul viewed the relationship of Spirit-guided Christians to God, but also how he understood the unique relationship of Jesus to God his Father.

# CHAPTER FIVE

# Glory Reflected
# on the Face of Christ
# (2 Cor 3:7–4:6)

One of the most sublime ways in which Paul summed up an effect of the Christ-event is found in a very complicated passage in 2 Corinthians 3–4, dealing with the veil on Moses' face.[1] Anyone who has wrestled with the flow of his thought in that passage is aware of the complications that attend it. It is easy enough to explain the effect of the Christ-event itself to which Paul subordinates his discussion in that passage, but it is another matter to unravel the threads of the discussion and to appreciate the images and motifs that are involved in it. No little part of the difficulty stems from the mode of argumentation that is found in this part of the Second Letter to the Corinthians; for it is surprising that Paul, in writing to such a Greek community, would indulge in the midrashic sort of argumentation that he employs there. One wonders whether the Corinthian Christians would have appreciated the subtlety of his argument, since it is so closely based on an Old Testament passage and utilizes figures and motifs that turn up in Palestinian Jewish writings.

This is, however, only a small part of the larger problem of the interpretation of the Corinthian correspondence; for it has always been a puzzle why the Aramaic acclamation *marana tha* should be preserved in 1 Cor 16:22,[2] or why there should be passages with a heavy midrashic element in these letters (e.g. 1 Cor 10:1–5; 2 Cor 3:7–4:6),[3] or with testimonia-composition

(2 Cor 6:14–7:1),[4] or with allusions to Palestinian Jewish angelology (1 Cor 11:10).[5] One would not expect such elements to be appreciated in Christian communities of such a Gentile background.

Part of the answer to this puzzle has been to appeal to the broken inscription found at Corinth that mentions a [*syn*]*agōgē Hebrai*[*ōn*], "Synagogue of the Hebrews,"[6] revealing that Jews had indeed settled in Corinth, or to appeal to the activity of Apollos in Corinth, "a Jew . . . a native of Alexandria, . . . well versed in the Scriptures" (Acts 18:24; cf. 1 Cor 1:12; 3:4–6,22; 4:6), not to mention the theory of some interpreters that Hellenistic Jews of Corinth would have sent to Paul an interpretation of the veil passage from Exodus and that he would have corrected it.[7] In any case, the very midrashic or Jewish elements that seem to be found in certain passages of the Corinthian correspondence have been part of the reason for arguing that Paul was aware of the mixed character of the Corinthian Christian community. The puzzle remains, but it provides the background for the Jewish motif which is present in 2 Corinthians 3–4, when considered in the light of certain Qumran texts.

Even without the consideration of the Qumran material, the passage had already been regarded as a "Christian midrash" on Exodus 34. It was apparently first so characterized by H. Windisch;[8] and others such as H. Lietzmann, C. J. A. Hickling, J. D. G. Dunn, and A. T. Hanson have repeated this characterization. I consider this assessment correct. It is one of the few passages in the New Testament that is clearly midrashic in the strict sense (others being Galatians 3–4; 1 Corinthians 10 [in part]; and Hebrews 7). But rather than ascribe it to a pre-Pauline or anti-Pauline origin, I prefer with H. Lietzmann[9] to regard it as composed by Paul for another occasion and inserted into this place in 2 Corinthians.

A further preliminary remark should be made about the effect of the Christ-event that Paul discusses in this passage. It is not my main concern to develop the background of the image employed; but a word should be said about it, since it bears on the major affirmation of the passage. Paul affirms that as a result of the Christ-event the person who puts faith in Christ Jesus is gradually "transformed" (*metamorphoumetha*) by degrees of glory reflected on and from the face of Christ. This effect of the Christ-event has been associated with the "new creation" in Pauline theology,[10] and yet it is not the same image, nor does it share the same background. "New creation" (Gal 6:15; 2 Cor 5:17) is an image drawn from Paul's Old Testament background: what God did in the beginning as he created the world and made Adam and Eve he now does again in a new way, creating a new humanity in Christ Jesus.

Perhaps associated with that image, but really distinct from it is another, *metamorphōsis,* the "transformation" of human beings in Christ Jesus. This image is found almost exclusively in 2 Cor 3:7–4:6,[11] especially in 3:18, where Paul says that we are all "being changed into his likeness from one degree of glory to another" (*tēn autēn eikona metamorphoumetha apo doxēs eis doxan*). Now despite the heavy use of Old Testament and Jewish motifs in the passage, derived mostly from the Moses story in Exod 34:27–35, the image itself is taken over from the Greco-Roman world. Neither the noun *metamorphōsis* nor the verb *metamorphoun* is found in the LXX.[12] It is a mythological figure, taken over from Greco-Roman metamorphosis literature. Tales of transformation are as old as Homer in the Greek world (*Iliad* 2. 319); and in Alexandrian times it became popular to make collections of such legends: e.g., the *Heteroioumena* of Nicander (2d cent. B.C.), the *Metamorphoses* of Ovid (A.D. 1), or the *Golden Ass* of Apuleius (2d cent. A.D.). Paul does not hesitate to take up such a mythological figure and apply it to the Christ-event. But, as this passage in 2 Corinthians makes clear, he has suffused the Greco-Roman image with Jewish, Old Testament, and Palestinian motifs; he uses it with the aid of his midrashic development of the Moses story.

The main argument in support of his view of the Christ-event as a transformation of the Christian is based on the Moses story in Exodus 34, but some features of it are dependent on other literature too. Among these is not only the allusion to Gen 1:3 (in 2 Cor 4:6), but also the use of a Palestinian motif which can now be illustrated from Qumran literature. My purpose is to bring to the attention of others the latter motif. But because Paul's discussion in this passage is complicated, I must set forth (I) the way in which the Pauline argument is presented as a whole. I shall (II) explain the Palestinian Jewish motif that is parallel to that argument. Thus my discussion will fall into two main parts.

## I. The Pauline Argument in 2 Cor 3:7–4:6

The section of the letter in which this paragraph appears seeks to express Paul's gratitude for the reconciliation with the Corinthian community that has taken place in spite of the troubles that he has had with it, mainly because of opponents who have spoken out against him there. This part of the letter is not easy to understand, because details in it refer to Paul's personal experience and are only vaguely or cryptically presented. For instance, why should Paul bring up the matter of a letter of recommendation, the topic with which chap. 3 begins? Was there some earlier difficulty about a letter of recommendation? Had he sent one to Corinth? Or was he challenged to produce one? If he had been, it is at best a conjecture made today, since Paul's allusions to it are cryptic and the facts escape us. In any case, the context into which he fits his midrashic interpretation of Exodus 34 is one in which he disclaims the need for a letter written on his behalf to the Corinthian community. His initial acceptance there and his preaching to the Corinthians have already produced self-vindicating results, as is attested by the experience of the Corinthians themselves.

[1]Are we beginning to commend ourselves again? Or do we need, as some do, letters of recommendation to you, or from you? [2]You yourselves are our letter of recommendation, written on your hearts, to be known and read by all. [3]You show that you are a letter from Christ delivered by us, written not in ink but with the Spirit of the living God, not on tablets of stone, but on tablets of human hearts. [4]Such is the confidence that we have through Christ toward God. [5]Not that we are competent of ourselves to claim anything as coming from us; our competence is from God, [6]who has made us competent as ministers of a new covenant, not in a written code but in the Spirit; for the written code kills, but the Spirit gives life. [7]Now if the dispensation of death, carved in letters on stone, came with such glory that the Israelites could not look at Moses'

face because of its brightness, fading as this was, [8]will not the
dispensation of the Spirit be attended with greater glory? [9]For
if there was glory in the dispensation of condemnation, the
dispensation of righteousness must far exceed it in glory.
[10]Indeed, in this case, what once had glory has come to have
no glory at all, because of the glory that surpasses it. [11]For if
what faded away came with glory, what is permanent must have
much more glory.
[12]Since, then, we have such a hope, we are very bold, [13]not like
Moses, who put a veil over his face so that the Israelites might
not see the end of the fading glory. [14]But their minds were
hardened; for to this day, when they read the old covenant, that
same veil remains unlifted, since only through Christ is it taken
away. [15]Yes, to this day whenever Moses is read a veil lies over
their minds; [16]but when one turns to the Lord the veil is removed. [17]Now the Lord is the Spirit; and where the Spirit of
the Lord is, there is freedom. [18]And we all, with unveiled face,
beholding the glory of the Lord, are being changed into his
likeness from one degree of glory to another; for this comes
from the Lord who is the Spirit.
[4:1]Therefore, having this ministry by God's mercy, we do not
lose heart . . . . [3]Even if our gospel is veiled, it is veiled only
to those who are perishing. [4]In their case the god of this world
has blinded the minds of those who do not believe, to keep them
from seeing the light of the gospel of the glory of Christ, who
is the likeness of God. [5]For what we preach is not ourselves,
but Jesus Christ as Lord, with ourselves as your servants for
the sake of Jesus. [6]For it is the God who said, "Let light shine
out of darkness," who has shone in our hearts, to give the light
of the knowledge of the glory of God in the face of Christ.

The puzzling element in this passage is how Paul can begin
with such a trivial matter as a letter of recommendation and
pass from it to the involved discussion about the veil on Moses'
face, and from that to the sublime theology of the glory or
splendor of the creator-God reflected on the face of Christ.
What is operative here, and what is perhaps not noted often
enough, is the free association of ideas that runs through the
entire passage. The association is caused by catchword bonding,
in which one sense of a term suggests another, and so the argument proceeds. To a modern reader, accustomed (at least
implicitly) to a mode of reasoning that is either Aristotelian

or related to it, the argument used by Paul does not seem to proceed logically. It uses neither syllogism nor enthymeme. The argument seems to involve more than three terms, and the "supposition" of the second or third term often shifts, implying a multiplicity of nuances that amount to new terms.

Paul's mode of argumentation has sometimes been called "rabbinic logic" and has been compared loosely to the principle of *gĕzērāh šāwāh,* "inference by analogy." But, though Paul is not explaining one pentateuchal passage by another in which the same word occurs, the association involved in such analogical inference is not far removed from the free association in which he here indulges.[13] In any case, his mode of argumentation cannot be subjected to syllogistic analysis. Once this is realized, it is possible to set forth schematically six sets of association that are at work in the passage.

(1) The argument begins with the mention of no need of *systatikai epistolai,* "letters of recommendation,"[14] for the Corinthians themselves are his *epistolē,* "letter," written on your [= their] hearts (3:2). The addition of the last phrase (*engegrammenē en tais kardiais*) begins to change the sense of *epistolē.* This enables Paul to forget completely the idea of letters of recommendation written on papyrus or skin and to pass on to the nuance of something written on the heart. In using this phrase, Paul makes his first allusion to the Old Testament, either to Jer 31:33, where the prophet speaks of God's new covenant with Israel and of his law written on their hearts, or possibly to Ezek 11:19 or 36:26, where this prophet promises that God will put a new spirit into his people and give them a heart of flesh instead of a heart of stone. Both prophetic passages themselves allude to the giving of the law to Moses written on "tablets of stone" (Exod 34:12). This allusion enables Paul to play upon the nuance of something "written not with ink but with the Spirit of the living God, not on tablets of stone but on tablets of human hearts" (3:3). Thus Paul presents himself as God's messenger and representative, justifying his apostolate and his ministry of a universal gospel. Such is his qualification. But it is only the beginning of the free associations.

(2) The second association begins with the idea of something written, something having letters; this is no longer "letter" in

the sense of *epistolē,* but "letter" as *gramma(ta),* i.e. letters of the alphabet with which one writes a document. The Mosaic law was written on tablets of stone in Hebrew letters (*grammata*); and they are for Paul lifeless letters, the symbol of the "old covenant" (3:14), indeed, the letter that kills.[15] With them he compares the life-giving Spirit, the bringer of the "new dispensation." God has made Paul the competent dispenser of the "new covenant" of the Spirit (3:6); he is the new runner who carries a letter written by Christ on human hearts through the Spirit. What began as a letter of recommendation "delivered by us" (*diakonētheisa hyph' hēmōn*) has now become Paul himself, "a dispenser of a new covenant, not of the letter, but of the Spirit" (*diakonos kainēs diathēkēs, ou grammatos, alla pneumatos,* 3:6). This contrast is not one of polemics, as it is sometimes understood, but results from a shift in Paul's thinking. And the free association does not stop there.

(3) With a sort of *qal wa-ḥōmer* argument,[16] Paul now begins to contrast the "splendor" or "glory" (*doxa*) that attended the giving of the law to Moses with the splendor or glory attending the giving of the Spirit. With pejorative and unflattering terms he refers to the promulgation of the Mosaic law as a "dispensation of death" and "of condemnation" (*diakonia tou thanatou* [3:7]; *diakonia tēs katakriseōs* [3:9]), because it had been encoded in letters that kill and engraved on lifeless tablets of stone. Yet it was accompanied by such *doxa!* Here we must recall the details of Exod 34:27–35, which from this point on (3:7) becomes the basis of the midrash that Paul now develops; his allusions to this passage are quite formal and cannot be mistaken. The text of Exodus begins with God's command to Moses to make a second pair of stone tablets and continues:

> [27]The Lord said to Moses, "Write these words: in accordance with these words I have made a covenant with you and with Israel." [28]He was there with the Lord forty days and forty nights; he neither ate bread nor drank water. He wrote upon tablets the words of the covenant, the ten commandments. [29]When Moses came down from Mount Sinai with the two tablets of testimony in his hand, as he came down from the mountain, Moses did not know that the skin of his face shone (*dedoxastai hē opsis tou chrōmatos tou prosōpou*) because he had been talking with God. [30]When Aaron and all the people of Israel looked at Moses,

the skin of his face suddenly shone, and they were afraid to come near him. ³¹But Moses called to them; Aaron and all the leaders of the congregation returned to him, and Moses talked with them. ³²Afterward all the people of Israel came near, and he gave them in commandment all that the Lord had spoken with him on Mount Sinai. ³³When Moses had finished speaking with them, he put a veil (*kalymma*) on his face; ³⁴but whenever Moses went in before the Lord to speak with him, he took the veil off, until he came out. When he came out and told the people of Israel what he had been commanded, ³⁵the people of Israel saw Moses' face, that the skin of it shone (*dedoxastai*). Then Moses would put the veil on his face again, until he went in to speak with him.

Against the background of this story Paul finds the *doxa* attending the "new covenant" to be "surpassing" (*hyperballousa*), because it is "the dispensation of the Spirit," not of the letter. This *diakonia tou pneumatos* carries all the associations of his argument thus far, but the allusion to Exod 34:27–35 has now introduced the further nuance of *doxa,* which becomes the springboard for still other associations.

(4) "Splendor" or "glory" has nothing to do with a letter of recommendation or even with the letter/spirit contrast which Paul uses elsewhere in his letters (e.g. Rom 2:27–29). It is here seen as something sacred or divine, which was associated with the giving of the Mosaic law in letters on tablets of stone, the very law which Paul in Romans admits was "good, just, and holy" (7:12), indeed, even "spiritual" (Rom 7:14).¹⁷ There is, then, no difficulty in his saying here that it was attended with *doxa* (3:7).

Yet that *doxa* assumes another role, for it is something that frightens the Israelites, since the skin of Moses' face shone as a result of exposure to it. In this Paul follows the detail of Exod 34:30, asserting that the law came with such glory that the Israelites could not look at Moses' face because of its brightness (*dia tēn doxan,* 3:7). Thus the *doxa* that attended the giving of the law by the Lord has moved to the *doxa* reflected on Moses' face, and this is what frightens the Israelites.

Paul moves a step further, adding an element of his own, "the glory that was fading away" (*hē doxa hē katargoumenē*). This detail is not found in the story in Exodus, but it enables

Paul to introduce the idea of the "surpassing glory" of the new covenant. The free association has thus moved from Yahweh's glory attending the giving of the Torah, to the frightening glory reflected on Moses' face, to the passing glory that was fading away from that face, to the surpassing glory attending the new dispensation of the Spirit. So runs the concatenation of associations involving *doxa*.

(5) The frightening glory introduces the need of a veil, and the next set of (involved) associations has to do with it. When Moses descended from Mt. Sinai, he put a veil on his face. Exod 34:30 explains its purpose: lest the reflected glory continue to frighten the Israelites. In 3:7 Paul does not explain this use of the veil explicitly, being content merely to allude to it. Thus the first use of the veil for him is to hide the reflected glory of Yahweh lest it cause fright. The second use of the veil is derived from Paul's addition to the Exodus story: it is used to conceal from the Israelites the fact that the *doxa* that once attended the giving of the law was fading: "so that the Israelites might not see the end of the fading glory" (3:13), or possibly, according to some commentators, "the goal" or "the purpose" (*telos*) of the fading glory, that it had to fade in order to be surpassed.

But now a peculiar shift in Paul's thinking introduces a third use of the veil: it serves to hide Moses himself from the Israelites. Here the association implies that a veil, hanging before the face of someone, conceals that person from others. Thus Moses becomes hidden from the people. Fast upon the heels of this association, Paul adds yet a fourth use: those who gaze upon someone veiled do not see the hidden person, and so they are themselves like blind people. "For to this day, when they read the old covenant, that same veil remains . . . . Yes, to this day whenever Moses is read, a veil lies over their minds" (3:14-15). Here the associations tumble fast, one upon the other. What began as an instrument to conceal the glory of Yahweh from frightened Israelites has become an instrument that prevents Israelites from understanding Moses, as they read him.

(6) Lastly, the sense of Moses has changed in the passage. It began with Moses, the personal intermediary in the promulgation of the law (see Gal 3:20), as in Exodus 34; it ends with

"Moses," denoting the biblical writings ascribed to him. As in Acts 15:21, "Moses" is something that is read, viz. the law, promulgated by him.

Now this elaborate build-up of free associations enables Paul to make his real points, and they are three: (a) The veil is lifted or removed only through Christ (3:14). (b) Playing on the idea of Moses' removal of the veil whenever he would turn to "the Lord" (viz. Yahweh, Exod 34:34–35), Paul bluntly says, "But when one turns to the Lord, the veil is removed" (3:17). Here "the Lord" is clearly the risen Christ, whom he even calls "the Spirit," a formulation not unrelated to 1 Cor 15:45; Rom 1:4:[18] "Now the Lord is the Spirit." (c) The person who turns to the Lord in faith and accepts him as such gazes with unveiled face upon the glory of the risen Christ. This glory surpasses that of the old dispensation, because it succeeds in transforming the person so confronted into a Christian: "And we all, with unveiled face gazing on the glory of the Lord, are being changed into his likeness from one degree of glory to another; for this comes from the Lord who is the Spirit" (3:18).

Thus Paul has suffused the Greco-Roman image of *metamorphōsis* with details of a thoroughly Jewish, midrashic interpretation of Exod 34:27–35. But in chap. 3 he has not yet explained the origin of the *doxa;* for this we pass to chap. 4.

The first few verses of chap. 4 do not concern us; they are something of a digression (picking up on 3:6). The origin of the *doxa kyriou* is explained in vv. 3–6:

> [3]Even if our gospel is veiled, it is veiled only to those who are perishing. [4]In their case the god of this world has blinded the minds of the unbelievers, to keep them from seeing the light of the gospel of the glory of Christ, who is the likeness of God. [5]For what we preach is not ourselves, but Jesus Christ as Lord. For it is the God who said, "Let light shine out of darkness," who has shone in our hearts, to give the light of the knowledge of the glory of God in the face of Christ.

Here Paul treats his gospel somewhat like the second sense of "Moses," which we have just considered. It is something veiled only to those who may read it and who are affected by "the god of this world," who blinds them. They stand in contrast to the persons who are influenced by the creator-God, the source of all light and glory, who is even the source of the glory of the risen Christ himself. Now *doxa* is understood as something that has its ultimate source in the creator of Genesis. Paul alludes to Gen 1:3, as he paraphrases it, "Let light shine out of darkness," and thus refers to the creator as the source of the *doxa* that shines on the face of Christ as on a mirror.[19] Christ is thus the *eikōn*, "likeness," of the creator, and in turn reflects the same *doxa* onto the faces of those who turn to him, with unveiled faces. As one ray of glory after another is thus reflected first on the face of Christ and then on the face of the Christian, he or she is transformed by degrees. All this comes from the glory of the Father, who first brought forth light from darkness. The intermediary is now Christ, the image of the Father, the creator-God.

This metamorphosis is thus achieved through the *doxa kyriou*. In Rom 6:4 Paul says that "Christ was raised from the dead by the glory of the Father," and in Phil 3:10 he speaks of his longing to "know him (i.e. Christ) and the power of his resurrection." In the latter passage the "power" is not limited simply to the effect of the risen Christ on the believer, but means ultimately that power which brought about the resurrection of Jesus itself, which is nothing else but the "glory of the Father."[20] It is the same power with which Jesus is constituted Son of God as of the resurrection (Rom 1:4). All these passages reveal that for Paul the *dynamis* and *doxa* of the Father are the source of the risen life, the dynamo of Christian living. These are the undercurrents of his discussion in 3:18.

With this we may pass to the second main point of this paper.

## II. A Palestinian Jewish Motif Parallel to the Argument in 2 Corinthians 3–4

We have seen how Paul has suffused a Greco-Roman motif of metamorphosis with a midrashic development of the Moses story of Exodus 34 and with an allusion to Genesis 1. Another motif may well have colored his thinking. For the idea of God's glory shining on the face of the risen Christ and in turn being reflected on the face of those who turn to him finds a certain counterpart in some Qumran literature. Here we read about

God illumining the face of the Teacher of Righteousness or of the priests of the community, and about him/them, in turn, illumining the face of the Many in the community. The medium of illumination is, indeed, not the glory of God, as in 2 Corinthians 3–4, but some of the details provide an interesting parallel to Paul's argument. Four main passages may be considered: (1) 1QH 4:5–6. The Hebrew of this text reads as follows:

> ⁵'ôdĕkā 'ădônāy kî' ha'îrôtāh pānay librîtĕkāh ûm[in ]
> ⁶[        ]'ădôršĕkāh wĕkaššaḥar nākôn lĕ'ô[rtayi]m hôpa'tāh
> lî.²¹

⁵I praise you, Lord, for you have illumined my face with your covenant and f[rom        ] ⁶[        ] I will seek you; like the true dawn of morning, you have appeared to me for enlightenment.

In this instance, the illumination comes from the God of the covenant, i.e. the law of Moses, which is regarded as the source of light that illumines.²²

(2) 1QH 4:27–29. This text supplies the counterpart of the foregoing:

> ²⁷ûbî ha'îrôtāh pĕnê rabbîm wattigbar 'ad lĕ'ên mispār kî
> hôda'tanî bĕrāzê ²⁸pil'ăkāh ûbĕsôd pil'ăkāh higbartāh 'immādî
> wĕhaplî' lĕneged rabbîm ba'ăbûr kĕbôdĕkāh ûlĕhôdîā' ²⁹lĕkôl
> haḥayyîm gĕbûrôtĕkāh.²³

²⁷Through me you have illumined the faces of (the) Many, and you have shown yourself immeasurably strong. For you have given me knowledge through your wondrous mysteries, ²⁸and through your wondrous secrets you have manifested your might with(in) me; you have done wonders before (the) Many for the sake of your glory and to make known ²⁹your mighty acts to all the living.

(3) 1QSb 4:24–28. In the second appendix to the *Manual of Discipline* one finds a Blessing of the Priests, part of which reads:

> ²⁴. . . wĕ'attāh ²⁵kĕmal'ak pānîm bimĕ'ôn qôdeš likbôd 'ĕlôhê
> ṣĕbā'[ôt ta'ăbôd lĕ'ôlām wĕti]hyeh sābîb mĕšārēt bĕhêkal
> ²⁶malkût ûmappîl gôrāl 'im mal'ăkê pānîm wa'ăṣat yahad ['im
> qĕdôšîm] lĕ'ēt 'ôlām ûlĕkôl qiṣṣê neṣaḥ kî' ²⁷['ĕmet kôl

*mišpāṭāyw wîśîmĕkāh qôd[eš] bĕ'ammô ûlĕmā'ôr [gādôl lĕ'ôr]
lĕtēbēl bĕda'at ûlĕhā'îr pĕnê rabbîm* [28][bĕsēkel ḥayyîm
*wîśîmĕkāh] nēzer lĕqôdeš qodāšîm, kî' ['attāh tĕqud]daš lô
ûtĕkabbēd šĕmô wĕqôdāšāyw.*[24]

[24]. . . and as for you, [25][may you serve forever] like an angel
of the Presence in the holy abode of the glory of the God of
Hos[ts; and may you (ever)] be ministering about in (his) royal
[26]palace, casting (your) lot with the angels of the Presence and
(giving) counsel together with the Holy Ones for time everlasting
and for all ages in perpetuity. For [27][truth (characterizes) all]
his judg]ments, and may he make you a holy thin[g] among his
people and a [great] luminary [for the light] of the world in
knowledge, to shine upon the face of many [28][with the insight
of life]. [May he make you] something vowed to infinite holiness,
for [you are conse]crated to him, and you will glorify his name
and his Holy Ones!

(4) 1QS 2:2-4. The *Manual of Discipline* instructs the priests
of the community to bless all those of God's lot who walk
perfectly in all his ways:

[2]. . . *yĕbārēkĕkāh bĕkôl* [3]*ṭôb wĕyišmōrĕkāh mikkôl ra' wĕyā'îr
libbĕkāh bĕsēkel ḥayyîm wîhûnnĕkāh bĕda'at 'ôlāmîm* [4]*wĕyiśśā'
pĕnê ḥāsādāyw lĕkāh lišlôm 'ôlāmîm.*[25]

[2]. . . May (God) bless you with everything [3]good and keep you
from all evil; may he illumine your mind with the insight of life
and grace you with the knowledge of eternity! [4]May he lift up
his gracious countenance toward you for everlasting peace!

The specific image that Paul uses, that of the face of Christ
as a reflecting mirror, is not found in these Qumran passages,
but there are several features in them that share a similarity
and provide the Palestinian Jewish background for the image
that he is using.

*First,* there is the action of God causing light to shine on
the face either of the Teacher of Righteousness in the Thanksgiving Psalms (if that is the person who speaks in the first person
singular) or of the priests who are blessed and consecrated.
The same function is further attributed to the Teacher or the
priests who light up the faces of the Many (i.e. the members
of the community).

*Second,* the last passage speaks of the illumination of the heart rather than the face, because much of the phraselogy used there occurs in other passages; but it also reveals that its literary origin is the blessing of the sons of Aaron in Num 6:24–26: *yĕbārekĕkā Yahweh wĕyišmĕrékā / yā'ēr Yahweh pānāyw 'ēlékā wîḥunnékkā / yiśśā' Yahweh pānāyw 'ēlékā wĕyāśēm lĕkā šālôm,* "May the Lord bless you and keep you; / may the Lord make his face shine upon you and be gracious to you; / may the Lord lift up his face to you and give you peace." The face of God shining on his people is also found in Ps 31:17; 67:2. These are the Old Testament sources of the Qumran expressions.

*Third,* it is precisely in the Thanksgiving Psalms, col. 4, where the two aspects of the illumination are joined. G. Jeremias, in his monograph *Der Lehrer der Gerechtigkeit,* has made out a good case for the authorship of several of the psalms by the Teacher of Righteousness. He considers seven of the psalms to be the work of this teacher: 1QH 7:6–25; 2:1–19; 2:31–39; 4:5–5:4; 5:5–19; 5:20–7:5; 8:4–40.[26] The two first passages quoted above come from one of these. Thus the Teacher of Righteousness would consider his own countenance illumined by the light coming from God and understand his own countenance, in turn, as illumining the Many.[27]

*Fourth,* it is interesting to note in 1QH 4:5 that the purpose of God's illumination of the countenance of the Teacher is *librîtĕkāh,* "with your covenant." The context is unfortunately damaged, and we cannot be certain about the nuance associated with this illumination. But it is well known that the community considered itself as living in a new sense the *bĕrît 'El* (1QS 5:8; CD 5:1); in fact, Jeremiah's expression "new covenant" (*bĕrît ḥădāšāh,* 31:31 [LXX 38:31, *diathēkē kainē*]) is picked up and used expressly in CD 6:19 (cf. also 1QpHab 2:[3]). This was clearly a renewed understanding of the Mosaic covenant of old (see 1QS 5:7–9), to which the Pauline passage is not unrelated. It is one of the few places in his writings in which Paul alludes to the Mosaic covenant. True, he speaks here of "the old covenant" (3:14), and of it as a dispensation of death (3:7) or a dispensation of condemnation (3:9). They are scarcely terms that the members of the Qumran community would care to hear about; but it also reveals Paul's attempt to move beyond a more or less contemporary Jewish understanding of the "new covenant" to a form that is associated with the illumination of those who accept the gospel of Christ which he preaches (4:4). This is the illumination that comes from the dispensation that "surpasses" (3:10) the dispensation of old, the gospel of the glory of Christ, the "new covenant" of the Spirit, of which he has become the *diakonos* (3:6).

*Fifth,* there is also the mention of "glory" in two of the Qumran passages: *ba'ăbûr kĕbôdĕkāh,* "for the sake of your glory" (1QH 4:28); *bimĕ'ôn qôdeš likbôd 'ĕlôhê ṣĕbā'[ôt],* "in the holy abode of the glory of the God of Hos[ts]." This, however, is merely incidental, since there is no relation between the *kābôd* and the illumination. The latter is not attributed to the former. It does not even function as does the "splendor" in Exodus 34. In the Qumran context the illumination is rather suggested as coming from "a great luminary" (*mā'ôr gādôl*), an expression that may recall Gen 1:16; but it is not the same allusion to Genesis that Paul makes in 2 Cor 4:6, "Let light shine out of darkness" (cf. Gen 1:3).

*Finally,* the phrase in 1QS 2:3, *wĕyā'îr libbĕkāh bĕsēkel ḥayyîm,* "may he (God) illumine your heart with the insight of life," has an interesting parallel in 2 Cor 4:6, "It is the God who said, 'Let light shine out of darkness,' who has shone in our hearts to give the light of the knowledge of the glory of God that is on the face of Christ." The illumination that is given affects the heart and imparts knowledge of some sort. The Pauline expression is obviously more Christian in its connotation, but the association of the illumination of the heart with knowledge with that in the Qumran text is not to be missed.

We have, then, in these Qumran texts a motif of illumination, more specifically a motif of the divine illumination of the face or the heart of members of the community. Similarly, in 2 Corinthians 3–4 we have a developed form of such illumination, which Paul has filled out with the midrashic treatment of the Moses story of Exodus 34 and used to present an effect of the Christ-event as metamorphosis. The difference between the two uses of illumination is obvious. For Paul the crucial factor in the development is Christ as the image or mirror of the glory of the creator God. In the Qumran literature the crucial factor is the Mosaic law, for that is what illumines the face of the Teacher of Righteousness or of the priests and is the means by which he or they illumine the faces of the Many, i.e. with his or their esoteric interpretation of it.[28] Paul is reacting against the law, which has become for him "the written code" that kills, but in the Qumran community it brings the illumination; it is the source of "the insight of life" (1QS 2:3) or of "knowledge" (1QS 2:3; 1QSb 4:27).[29]

In an article on this Pauline passage, W. C. van Unnik once noted that vv. 17–18 have been "considered as one of the clearest expressions of Paul's mysticism, which according to many scholars was steeped in Hellenistic terminology and experience: transfiguration by vision. There is no other Pauline text which so clearly reveals his deepest experience and — according to some — his non-Jewish mode of thinking."[30] That it is an expression of Paul's mysticism can easily be admitted; that it is "clear" is another matter, as I have been trying to show. But that it is steeped solely in "Hellenistic terminology" needs considerable qualification. The motif of metamorphosis may be such; but the motif of what van Unnik calls "transfiguration by vision" is rooted rather in Palestinian Jewish motifs. At least, so I should prefer to explain it.

One last comment is in order. If Paul does make use of the mythical figure of metamorphosis, it is not to be understood crudely. The person who turns to the Lord with unveiled face and accepts the gospel of the glory of Christ is conceived of by Paul as being transformed by one degree after another of glory of the creator-God reflected on the face of Christ, who is the "image" of the Father. Paul never so expresses it that that person is transformed into Christ himself, as the pagan myths might suggest; rather, through that constant subjection to the reflected glory the person is gradually being transformed into a likeness of him. One may wonder how this image of the Christ-event fits in with other ideas of Paul about the union of the Christian and Christ ("in Christ," or "Christ lives in me," etc.). It may be that this image of transformation cannot be easily put together with the other ways of expressing such union; but that is in the long run part of the wealth of Pauline thinking. For they all constitute different ways of conceiving what van Unnik and others have called "Paul's mysticism."

This Pauline notion helped Greek patristic writers to develop their ideas on the progressive divinization (*theōsis*) of the Christian.

# CHAPTER SIX

# The Meaning of Kephalē in 1 Corinthians 11:3

The 1 Corinthians passage, in which Paul insists that a woman praying or prophesying in the Christian assembly should have her head covered (11:2–16), has been said to be "in its present form hardly one of Paul's happier compositions. The logic is obscure at best and contradictory at worst. The word choice is peculiar; the tone peevish."[1] On an earlier occasion I addressed myself to the interpretation of one of the difficult phrases in this passage,[2] and I now turn to another one in v. 3 because some recent discussion of this verse may be obscuring its basic thrust and because some evidence relevant to its meaning has not been considered.

It has to do with the sense in which Paul uses *kephalē* in this verse, which reads:

> *thelō de hymas eidenai hoti*
> *pantos andros hē kephalē ho Christos estin,*
> *kephalē de gynaikos ho anēr,*
> *kephalē de tou Christou ho theos.*

> But I want you to understand that
> the head of every man is Christ,
> the head of a woman is her husband,
> and the head of Christ is God. (*RSV*)

From this statement Paul goes on to construct an argument about the need for a head-covering when a woman prays or prophesies in the public Christian assembly. Part of the problem is that Paul uses *kephalē* in the literal sense of the physical, anatomical "head" in vv. 4,5,7,10, but in v. 3 (and according to some commentators in the second instance of v. 4) he uses it in a metaphorical sense. But the problem is, in what metaphorical sense is it used in v. 3?

## I. Recent Discussion

Apparently J. Weiss was the first to toy with the idea that v. 3 might be a gloss on vv. 4–5, but even he had to recognize that v. 7 later played on the sense of v. 3.[3] More recently, W. O. Walker, Jr. has considered not only this verse, but all of vv. 2–16 to be an interpolation—indeed, an interpolation of three originally separate and distinct pericopae of non-Pauline composition (A: vv. 3,8–9,11–12; B: vv. 4–7,10,13,16; C: vv. 14–15).[4] One of Walker's reasons for distinguishing v. 3 from what follows in vv. 4,5,7,10 is precisely the metaphorical use of *kephalē* in v. 3 and its literal sense in the following verses. Thus Paul would be spared a charge of unhappy composition. Though G. W. Trompf subsequently insisted on the unity of vv. 3–16, he too recognized "that the whole passage sits ill at ease in the context of 1 Cor 10:1–11:34" and argued strongly for its interpolation into the original text (even though he remained undecided whether the excursus on head-covering came "from Paul or not").[5] Still later, L. Cope argued for the Pauline composition of v. 2 and limited the interpolation to vv. 3–16: the best argument for their interpolated character was that they were "suspect *in any context* in a Pauline letter" (his emphasis).[6]

In a number of articles, J. Murphy-O'Connor has not only insisted—rightly, in my opinion—on the unity of vv. 3–16, but also on their Pauline authorship.[7] He has done much to present a coherent interpretation of this difficult Pauline passage, but one aspect of his interpretation still creates a problem, the meaning of *kephalē* in v. 3 (and possibly of the second occurrence of it in v. 4). Murphy-O'Connor has been influenced mainly by R. Scroggs, who has translated v. 3 as follows:

I want you to know that
every man's source is Christ,
the source of woman is man,
the source of Christ is God.[8]

Scroggs claimed that "in normal Greek usage *kephalē* does not mean lordship, and while the word is sometimes used in the LXX to translate *r'ōš* [*sic*] when the Hebrew word carries the connotation of chief or leader, the more common word for that meaning is *archōn* or *archēgos*."[9] Scroggs later returned to a discussion of the meaning of *kephalē*, asserting that the article in *TWNT* on it does not suggest that "the word ever had such a metaphorical meaning in Greek literature" and that Liddell-Scott-Jones "does not even give it as a sub-category within the metaphorical usages."[10] Scroggs labels the LXX translator who rendered Hebrew *rō'š* as *kephalē* in the sense of "leader" as "wooden-headed or sleepy . . . ; this is not the usual procedure."[11] According to him, in the LXX of Numbers *kephalē* occurs as a translation of Hebrew *rō'š* nine times, of which eight have the literal meaning "head" (of a person or animal), and once (5:7 [read 6:7]) it is used metaphorically to mean "self." But *archōn* translates *rō'š*, "leader, ruler," seven times, and *archēgos,* four times.

Murphy-O'Connor has pressed beyond Scroggs, again maintaining that *kephalē* connoting "supremacy" or "authority" is not attested in profane Greek.[12] He admits that *kephalē* appears 281 times in the LXX as the translation of Hebrew *rō'š*. This Hebrew word occurs twenty-five times in Exodus, and the LXX renders it regularly by *kephalē* when used in the literal sense, but not in the three texts where *rō'š* means "ruler." Similarly, in 1 Samuel *kephalē* occurs in the literal sense thirteen times (out of twenty-two), but in the one instance where *rō'š* means "ruler," it is translated *hēgoumenos*. Murphy-O'Connor grants that ms. A of LXX Judg 10:18; 11:8,9,11 uses *kephalē* for *rō'š*, "leader, ruler," but notes that ms. B has *archōn* for Judg 10:18; 11:8,9, whereas it uses *kephalē* in 11:11. Though Murphy-O'Connor admits that his survey is "incomplete," he believes that it is

sufficiently based to show that the metaphorical meanings of *rō'š* and *kephalē* did not overlap completely, and that *kephalē* was inappropriate to render *rō'š* when this term connoted "authority." *Kephalē* does appear for *rō'š* = "ruler" in 2 Sam 22:44, but this single exception (even Homer nods!) does not change the picture. There is simply no basis for the assumption that a Hellenized Jew would instinctively give *kephalē* the meaning "one having authority over someone."[13]

Thus has Murphy-O'Connor stated the case, and he too prefers to translate *kephalē* in 1 Cor 11:3 as "source."[14]

Whether it be a case of Homer nodding or of a wooden-headed or sleepy translator, is it correct to speak of a "single exception," when one is dealing with the use of *kephalē* in the LXX or in other Greek literature? (After all, Murphy-O'Connor has admitted that *kephalē*, "ruler, leader," is also found in Judg 10:18; 11:8,9,11, at least in ms. A.) But there is more to be said on this subject.

## II. Further Evidence Bearing on the Use of *kephalē* in 1 Corinthians 11

Let us leave aside for the moment the question whether *kephalē* ever connotes "supremacy" or "authority, leadership" elsewhere in Greek literature. In general, in the Old Testament the Hebrew word *rō'š* means (1) "head" in the literal, anatomical sense (Gen 40:16–17 [of a man]; 3:15 [of an animal]); (2) "top" (Gen 8:5 [of a mountain]); (3) "head = chief" (Judg 10:18; 11:8,9,11); (4) "beginning, source" (Gen 2:10 [of rivers]; Judg 7:19 [of watches of the night]); (5) "sum" (Exod 30:12 [in a census]); and (6) "division, company" (Judg 7:16 [of an army]). It is no surprise that the LXX renders the first two of these meanings by *kephalē* either "head" or "top." Nor is it a surprise that *rō'š* in the sense of "beginning, source" is usually rendered by *archē* (or some cognate of it).[15] The problem is whether a "Hellenistic Jew" would rightly give *kephalē* the meaning "one having authority over someone else."

Apart from the LXX passages already mentioned by Scroggs or Murphy-O'Connor where *kephalē* does occur in this sense (Judg 10:18; 11:8,9,11 [at least in ms. A]; 2 Sam 22:44), we may consider the following passages:

(1) In Isaiah 7 the prophet counsels Ahaz, the King of Judah, about the war plotted against him by Aram and Ephraim. Part of Isaiah's words to Ahaz (vv. 8–9) runs as follows:

⁸ᵃkî rō'š 'ărām dammeśeq wĕrō'š dammeśeq rĕṣîn . . . ⁹wĕrō'š 'eprayim šōmrôn ben rĕmalyāhû.

In the *RSV* these lines are translated:

For the head of Syria is Damascus,
and the head of Damascus is Rezin . . .
And the head of Ephraim is Samaria,
and the head of Samaria is the son of Remaliah.

These verses, however, are rendered in the LXX as follows:

*all' hē kephalē Aram Damaskos . . .*
*kai hē kephalē Ephraim Somorōn,*
*kai hē kephalē huios tou Rhomeliou.*

The LXX does not translate the second part of v. 8a, but it clearly renders Hebrew *rō'š*, "head, chief,"[16] in the other three instances by *kephalē*. Now this Old Testament passage is not an exact parallel to Paul's words in 1 Cor 11:3, but no one can fail to miss the similarity in the use of *kephalē* in both passages or the bearing that this LXX text has on the meaning of the Pauline verse.

(2) In Jeremiah 31 the prophet tells of the homecoming of the remnant of Israel. In v. 7 he says:

*ronnû lĕya'ăqōb śimḥāh wĕṣahălû bĕrō'š haggôyim*

As the *RSV* puts it:

Sing aloud with gladness for Jacob,
and raise shouts for the chief of the nations.

This is rendered in the LXX as follows (38:7):

*Euphranthēte kai chremetisate epi kephalēn ethnōn.*

In this case it is not a question of the "head" of persons, but of nations; yet the notion of supremacy or authority is surely present, and expressed by *kephalē*.

(3) In 1 Kgs 21:12 the Hebrew text reads:

*wĕhōšîbû 'et-nābôt bĕrō'š hā'ām.*

This may be translated:

And they set up Naboth at the head of the people.

The LXX renders the sentence thus (20:12):

*kai ekathisan ton Nabouthai en kephalē tou laou.*[17]

Here both *rō'š* and *kephalē* have the nuance of prominence of place or position of authority.

(4) We have already mentioned 2 Sam 22:44 above, as Murphy-O'Connor's "single exception," but one should also note the half verse that follows the part quoted by him. In the Hebrew, 22:44bc runs as follows:

*tišmĕrēnî lĕrō'š gôyim 'am lō'-yāda'tî ya'abdûnî*

You preserve me as the head of the nations; people that I do not know will serve me.

This is rendered by the LXX thus:

*phylaxeis me eis kephalēn ethnōn, laos hon ouk egnō edouleusan moi.*

Though the LXX alters the tense of the verbs, the last half of the verse, which speaks of service of the people, makes it clear that *kephalē* is here used with the connotation of "authority" or "supremacy."

(5) The same connotation is present when persons are referred to as the "head" (*rō'š*) and the "tail" (*zānāb*); see Deut 28:13,44; Isa 9:13–14 (in this instance the LXX uses *kephalē* in v. 13 and explains it as *archē* in v. 14); 19:15 (here the LXX has *kephalēn kai ouran* for Hebrew *rō'š wĕzānāb*, whereas the following phrase *kippāh wĕ'agmōn*, "palm branch or reed," becomes in the Greek *archēn kai telos*).

Now these examples from the LXX show that *kephalē* has been used in a good number of instances to connote "authority" or "supremacy." I do not deny that *rō'š*, when used in the sense of "leader, ruler," is often rendered in the LXX by either *archōn* or *archēgos,* but the evidence adduced above shows that a Hellenistic Jew could instinctively use *kephalē* as a proper expression for such authority.

The above evidence may be sufficient to show that Paul in 1 Cor 11:3 could use *kephalē* in this Hellenistic Jewish sense to designate preeminence or authority. But there is further evidence from Philo that must be considered. True, in one instance Philo uses *kephalē* in the sense of "source," when he speaks of Esau "as the head of the living body, the progenitor of all the members mentioned" (*De Cong. erud. gratia* 12 §61). But he does use *kephalē* on several occasions in the sense of "leader" or "ruler," i.e. in the metaphorical sense of preeminence or authority.

(1) Philo clearly regards the head as a ruler:

> *kephalēn men toinyn allēgorountes phamen einai psychēs ton hēgemona noun.*

> "Head" we interpret allegorically to mean the mind, the ruling part of the soul. (*De somn.* 2.31 §207)[18]

(2) Philo speaks of Ptolemy II Philadelphus as one who was outstanding among the Ptolemies and expresses it thus:

> *genomenos kathaper en zōō to hēgemoneuon kephalē tropon tina tōn basileōn*

> being, as the head is the leading part in a living body, in some sense the head of kings [of the Ptolemaic dynasty]. (*De vita Mosis* 2.5 §30)

It should be noted in these first two instances that Philo is aware of using *kephalē* in a figurative sense: "allegorically," "in some sense."

(3) In still another instance Philo makes clear what he means by the relation of the head to the body:

> . . . *tēn tou sōmatos hēgemonian hē physis anēpse kephalē charisamenē.*

> Nature has conferred the leadership of the body on the head. (*De spec. leg.* 3.33 §184)

Note how in these three instances some form of *hēgemōn* is used.

(4) Lastly, I cite the following:

*ean men oun heis anēr tynchanē toioutos ōn en polei, tēs poleōs hyperanō phaneitai, ean de polis, tēs en kyklō chōras, ean de ethnos, epibēsetai pasin ethnesin hōsper kephalē sōmati tou periphainesthai charin, ouch hyper eudoxias mallon ē tēs tōn horōntōn ōpheleias.*

So then if one such man be found in a city—will appear superior to the city—or if a city (so appears) to the country roundabout, or if one nation will stand above all (other) nations, as a head above a body, to be conspicuous all about, (so it will be) not for (its own) glory, but for the benefit of those who behold it. (*De praem. et poenis* 19 §114)[19]

Finally, two further occurrences of *kephalē,* "leader," may be considered. At one point in his *Jewish War* Josephus is speaking about Jerusalem, comparing it with the country (*tēs chōras*) and outlying towns (*tōn exōthen poleōn*), and he calls it *tēn kephalēn holou tou ethnous,* "the head of the whole nation" (4.4.3 §261; cf. 3.3.5 §54). Again, in the *Shepherd of Hermas,* when Hermas requests that the shepherd of punishment depart from his house, he is told that he must suffer because of the great iniquity and sin committed by his family: . . . *ean mē sy hē kephalē tou oikou thlibēs,* "unless you, the head of the household, be afflicted" (*Sim.* 7.3). To these two instances, which come from fairly contemporary Greek, I may add one from a later writer Athanasius, which does not seem to be composed in dependence on some New Testament passage. He refers to some bishops as *kephalai tosoutōn ekklēsiōn,* "heads of such great churches" (*Apol. II contra Arianos* 89 [PG 25.409A]). The last examples may not be taken from "profane Greek literature," but none of them seems to be modelled on the use of *kephalē* in Col 2:10; Eph 1:22; 4:15; 5:23b, where many interpreters would admit that *kephalē* does connote authority or supremacy.

The upshot of this discussion is that a Hellenistic Jewish writer such as Paul of Tarsus could well have intended that *kephalē* in 1 Cor 11:3 be understood as "head" in the sense of authority or supremacy over someone else. This would mean that the opinion espoused by such commentators as those mentioned by J. Murphy-O'Connor (J. Weiss, A. Robertson and

A. Plummer, H. D. Wendland, B. Allo, J. Héring, H. Lietzmann, W. G. Kümmel, and F. W. Grosheide) is not as
unsubstantiated as might be thought in recent discussion of
this text.

Consequently, I should prefer to translate v. 3 in the following way:

> But I want you to understand that
> Christ is the head of every man,[20]
> man is the head of a woman,
> and God is the head of Christ.

The next edition of the *Greek-English-Lexicon* of Liddell-Scott-
Jones will have to provide a sub-category within the metaphorical uses of *kephalē* in the sense of "leader, ruler."[21] Lastly,
it should be clear that the "head" as the leading part of a living
body is not the anachronism that S. Bedale once thought it
was.[22] When Philo calls it the ruling part of the soul, he is
not saying something that would be unintelligible to Paul of
Tarsus.[23]

# CHAPTER SEVEN

# The Christological Hymn of Philippians 2:6–11

All readers of the New Testament are aware of the hymn that Paul has inserted into his discussion in chap. 2 of his letter to the Philippians. It is an important contribution to his understanding of Christ Jesus and a significant element of his christological teaching. It makes its own contribution to the argument of the letter that he is sending to his beloved community of followers.

It was apparently Johannes Weiss who first noted the "rhetorical structure" of Phil 2:6–11, calling attention to its "rhythmic and symmetric" parallelism of four clauses in vv. 6–8 and four in vv. 9–11.[1] Others subsequently sought to divide the passage into strophes and verses,[2] but it remained for Ernst Lohmeyer *1928* to analyze the passage as a pre-Pauline hymn, a position which most interpreters have since followed. He presented it in his commentary on the Epistle to the Philippians,[3] and devoted a separate monograph to the full discussion of this christological passage.[4] Subsequently, R. P. Martin refined Lohmeyer's treatment in a further important study.[5] *1967*

The passage in Philippians 2 is notorious for the problems that it raises, and it is not my purpose to rehearse all of them here. Among them, however, are two basic questions that may tolerate further discussion. The first has to do with its possible Aramaic original, and the second with its structure; but these questions are really interrelated. My discussion will, then, fall into three parts: (I) the Aramaic background of Phil 2:6–11; (II) the structure of Phil 2:6–11; and (III) the meaning and purpose of the hymn.

## I. The Aramaic Background
## of Philippians 2:6–11

Though Lohmeyer had analyzed the passage as a pre-Pauline psalm or hymn, which he divided into two strophes of three verses each, he did not try to retrovert the Greek text into Aramaic or Hebrew. He did, however, consider its Semitic background and compared it with passages in the Old Testament prophets and psalms (especially with verses of three accents), and with what he called the "basic form of Aramaic poetry," which he found to be present in the Son of Man hymn(s) in the Book of Daniel.[6] But he considered the words *epouraniōn kai epigeiōn kai katachthoniōn,* "of those in heaven, on earth, and under the earth," to be unthinkable in a Semitic language and eventually concluded that the poem was originally written in Greek by a poet whose mother-tongue was Semitic — in other words, it is a "Jewish-Christian psalm."[7]

Lohmeyer set forth the Greek text of Phil 2:6–11 in the following two strophes of three verses each:

(1)  [6][Ho] en morphē theou hyparchōn
     ouch harpagmon hēgēsato
     to einai isa theō
(2)  [7]alla heauton ekenōsen
     morphēn doulou labōn
     en homoiōmati anthrōpōn genomenos
(3)  kai schēmati heuretheis hōs anthrōpos
     [8]etapeinōsen heauton
     genomenos hypēkoos mechri thanatou
     [thanatou de staurou]
(4)  [9]dio kai ho theos hyperypsōsen auton
     kai echarisato autō
     to onoma to hyper pan onoma
(5)  [10]hina en tō onomati Iēsou pan gony kampsē
     epouraniōn kai epigeiōn kai katachthoniōn

(6)  [11]*kai pasa glōssa exomologēsetai*
   *hoti Kyrios Iēsous Christos*
   *eis doxan theou patros.*[8]

But Lohmeyer did not convince everyone. W. Michaelis
would admit only that Lohmeyer had shown that the passage
as a whole has a "poetic schema" in its "2 x 3 three-liners," but
noted that the lines are not always governed by three accents.[9]
E. Käsemann denied strongly that Phil 2:6–11 had been derived
from a Jewish Christian source and found it instead marked
by contemporary Hellenistic thinking.[10] Furthermore, F. W.
Beare went so far as to assert that there is no "good reason
to hold that the hymn is a translation from Aramaic (as does
Lohmeyer [?]) and to seek to throw light on its meaning through
the reconstruction of the hypothetical Aramaic expressions."[11]
One can agree with some of this criticism of Lohmeyer, especially his discussion of various aspects of the underlying
theology of the hymn as he reconstructs it in his monograph;
but Lohmeyer's discussion of the structure of the hymn was
an important contribution. If a few scholars have gone beyond
him in even trying to retrovert the christological hymn into
Aramaic, that too marks the significance of his contribution.

In a review of Lohmeyer's commentary and monograph,
W. K. Lowther Clarke not only hailed Lohmeyer's analysis and
interpretation of the hymn but also included a "transliteration
of a rendering into Galilean Aramaic of the supposed hymn,"
composed by P. P. Levertoff.[12] Levertoff's rendering of the
passage runs as follows:

I.  1. *Bidmúto de-elåha itóhi*
    2. *Wehåshba lo håwa leshalåla*
    3. *Itóhi le-péḥma de-elåha.*
II. 1. *Ela sårik we-hípshit et náphshe*
    2. *Udemúta de-åbda nåsba*
    3. *Be-tzílma de-ínsha itóhi;*
III. 1. *Ek bar-nasha ishtàkaḥ*
    2. *We-náphshe shåphal we-måkaḥ*
    3. *Adma le-mótha ishtáma* (*Mota de-tzeliba*)
IV. 1. *Al-kén agbéhe eláha*
    2. *We-yáheb lo shéma sagíha*
    3. *De-gebíha mikól shemáhin;*

V.  1.  *De-bishéma de-Yeshúa*
    2.  *Tikrá kol bírka*
    3.  *De-bishemáya u-be-ára we-dele-táhat de-ára*
VI.  1.  *We-kól lishán nóde*
    2.  *Yeshúa mashíha hu mára*
    3.  *Le-shúbha de-eláha abúhi*

This transcription was subsequently set in unpointed Hebrew type by R. P. Martin in his monograph on the hymn, but he mistakenly marks off the Pauline gloss, "death upon a cross," as the first line of verse IV, thus differing from Levertoff.[13]

Eventually P. Grelot turned to the question of the Aramaic background of this christological hymn. He judged Levertoff's rendering of it into Aramaic to be "très critiquable," and wondered about the dialect of Aramaic used in the retroversion.[14] Grelot showed that every verse in Levertoff's two strophes contained anomalous hebraisms, syracisms, and outright mistakes. He might also have mentioned that Levertoff inexplicably put accents on what would be shewas or reduced vowels in order to achieve the three-accent lines, and did not succeed even at that, since line V/2 has only two accents in his transcription.

Grelot also recognized that Levertoff, whose transcription was called by Lowther Clarke "Galilean Aramaic," was heavily influenced by the Peshitta and by readings in the Christian Palestinian lectionary. Grelot, however, rightly insisted that a retroversion of the hymn merited the effort, but that it had to be undertaken according to a form of the language at a proper stage of its development. He mentioned as a possibility the use of the form of Aramaic found in the pre-classical Old Syriac inscriptions from the Edessene area,[15] but actually preferred to relate the hymn to the language of the early Jewish-Christian communities of Judea. For him, they would have used the form of Aramaic spoken in Palestine in the first century and attested in "the Palestinian targum," or in the "literary 'classical' language" analogous to that of Daniel and Qumran texts (such as 11QtgJob, 1QapGen, 4QTLevi [CTLevi], 4QprNab, 4QEn). This was clearly a move in the right direction, even though I should hesitate to classify the Aramaic of the so-called Palestinian targum[16] with what he calls the "literary 'classical' language" of the aforementioned Palestinian texts, which otherwise come from the last two centuries B.C. and the first A.D. But in his retroversion of the hymn into Aramaic, Grelot has also made use of words attested in the Christian Palestinian lectionaries.[17] The use of this form of Aramaic is obviously better than the use of the Peshitta, since the former is at least Western Aramaic, whereas the latter is Eastern Aramaic and for that reason inadmissible. Grelot has not only retroverted the hymn into Aramaic but has also defended his choice of words, forms, and syntax with the aforementioned Aramaic texts.

If I find fault with some details in Grelot's retroversion, it is because parts of the hymn could be better rendered into contemporary Palestinian Aramaic. D. J. Harrington and I once gathered some 150 texts, often fragmentary or of short length, from the period concerned, and some of the material would aid in translating the christological hymn into such Aramaic.[18] But obviously, if some of the vocabulary of the Greek hymn finds no correspondence in contemporary Aramaic of the first century A.D. or in earlier Aramaic, then one may be forced to turn to forms of a later period of the language, *faute de mieux*.[19]

Grelot has retroverted the *Kyrios*-hymn into a form both in Hebrew characters and a roman transcription. His vocalized transcription runs as follows:[20]

(6) *bi-ṣelem 'ēlāhā 'îtôhî*
    *wᵉlâ ḥᵃtûf ḥᵃšab*
    
    *kᵉwāt 'ēlāhā lᵉmihwê*
    (or: *dî lehᵉwê kᵉwāt 'ēlāhā*)

(7) *'ellâ haddeq garmeh*
    *ûṣelem 'ebèd nāsib*

    *bi-dᵉmût 'enāš hawâ*
    *ûbᵉḥézû mištᵉkah ki-gᵉbar*
(8) *hašpil garmeh*
    *wᵉšamô' hᵃwâ 'ad mawtâ*
    (*mawtâ dî ṣᵉlîbetâ*)

(9) *lāken 'of 'ēlāhā rômᵉmeh*
    *wiyᵉhab leh šᵉmâ*
    *dî 'ellâ min kàl šum*

(10) *'al dibrat dî bi-šᵉmeh di-yéšû'*
     *tikra' kàl bérèk*
         (*dî bi-šᵉmayyâ ûbᵉ'ar'â*
         *ûli-tᵉḥôt 'ar'â*)

(11)                          *wᵉkàl liššān yôdê*
  *dî māre' yéšû' mᵉšîḥâ*        *li-yᵉqāreh dî 'élāhā 'abbâ.*[21]

My immediate concern is to see whether one can relatively
easily translate the Greek christological hymn into Aramaic
of a form that would resemble the contemporary Palestinian
dialect, prescinding from the question of structure.

Two comments, however, have to precede the attempt at
retroversion. *First,* practically all commentators on this passage
regard *thanatou de staurou,* "death upon a cross" (v. 8) as a
Pauline addition to the adopted hymn. Both Levertoff and
Grelot reckon with that addition too, but they nevertheless offer
a translation of the phrase, which encounters the immediate
difficulty that there is no word for "cross" attested in contemporary Aramaic. Both use a form of *ṣᵉlîbā'.* But if it is really
a Greek addition, then why try to include it in the Aramaic
form? *Second,* many interpreters also recognize that *epouraniōn kai epigeiōn kai katachthoniōn* are compound Greek
nouns and occur in a line that goes beyond the length of others
in the hymn; hence they too are often regarded as a Greek
addition to the Aramaic original. We have already noted
Lohmeyer's opinion of these words. But, as Grelot has noted,
though the compound nouns as such are untranslatable in
Aramaic, there is the combination of *dî* with prepositional
phrases that remarkably well captures the sense of the line. In
this case I am retaining it as part of the original.

My attempt to retrovert the passage of Phil 2:6–11 into
Aramaic would proceed thus:

*Verse 6*

*hu' biṣlēm 'ĕlāhā' 'îtôhî',* "He is in the form of God,"

The Greek text begins with the relative pronoun *hos,* to which
Aramaic *dî* would better correspond, but Lohmeyer realized
that the original hymn would scarcely so begin; he substituted
the definite article *ho* for *hos.* I agree with this, and thus begin
with Aramaic *hû'.* Grelot recognized that *morphē* in the LXX
of Dan 3:19 renders Aramaic *ṣĕlēm;* hence he rightly prefers
that to Levertoff's *dĕmût.* Since I use a form of *hăwā'* for

*genomenos* below, I prefer to follow Grelot in rendering *hyparchōn* with the particle *'îtay-*.

*wĕlā' ḥăšab šĕlāl,* "and he did not consider (as) booty"

As Grelot realized, the use of *'îtay-* for *hyparchōn* requires the addition of *wĕ-* at the beginning of this line. Since I can find no example of *lā'*, "not," preceding a direct object of a verb, I prefer to change the word-order and use *wĕlā' ḥăšab,* "and he did not consider." The Greek noun *harpagmos,* whose meaning is highly contested, is not found in the LXX, but this version has both *harpagma* and *harpagē.* The sense of the latter in Isa 10:2 might be suitable in this verse; there it renders Hebrew *šālāl.* Though *šĕlālā'* is unattested in contemporary Aramaic, it does occur regularly in later Aramaic. Levertoff made use of it, but Grelot has preferred a form of *ḥṭp,* which is used in both forms of the later Christian Palestinian lectionary (*ḥṭwp'*). The verb *ḥăšab* is well attested in contemporary Aramaic; see 11QtgJob 2:1 (= Hebrew 19:11), *wḥ[šbny],* which the LXX translates with a form of *hēgeisthai.*[22] See 1QapGen 2:1; *MPAT* 64:1.10,11,13; 2.5.

*lēmihwē' šāwê lē'lāhā',* "to be equal to God,"

This line explains *šĕlāl* of the preceding line; *lēmihwē',* "to be," functions as an epexegetical infinitive (cf. 11QtgJob 15:5; 4QTLevi ar 1:18). Because the adverb *isa* renders in the LXX the Hebrew *kĕ-* (Job 27:16), Grelot prefers to render it as *kēwāt* (cf. 11QtgJob 11:7). This preposition, however, is too weak for a translation of *to einai isa theō* (see BAGD 381; BDF §434.1). Hence I prefer to use the Aramaic participle *šāwê,* "equalling, being worth," which is attested in the Jason Tomb Inscription (*MPAT* 89:3); also in 5/6Hever Babatha Archive (line 13, *MPAT* 62:13); cf. Mur 72 ar 1:11 (*MPAT* 49:1.11); Dan 5:21; *AP* 15:8,11; *BMAP* 2:4; 4QEn astr[b] 7 iii 7. It is noteworthy that both forms of the Christian Palestinian lectionary also use *šw'.*

*Verse 7*

*bĕram 'ăšad napšēh,* "but he poured himself out"

Both Levertoff and Grelot have translated Greek *alla,* "but," by Aramaic *'ellā',* which is well attested in Late Aramaic, but not in the contemporary period of Middle Aramaic. The conjunction *brm,* "but," is found in 4QEnGiants^e 2:4 (*MPAT* 18:1.4), not to mention the earlier occurrences in Dan 2:28; 4:12,20; 5:17; Ezra 5:13. For the Greek verb *ekenōsen* Grelot uses *haddeq,* a form of *dqq,* "be empty," which has connotations that are hardly pertinent. However, the verb *'šd,* "pour out" (blood, tears) is found in Ahiqar 89; Pad 1:7; 11QtgJob 16:5 (= Hebrew 30:16), where it renders *tištappēk napšî,* "my soul is poured out." Grelot notes that the Greek verb *kenoun* is rare in the Greek versions of the OT and prefers to follow the Christian Palestinian lectionary's use of the aphel of *dqq,* but such a usage in the meaning of "empty" is unattested at this period. The Peshitta has at least the Eastern Aramaic cognate *sarreq* of *sry[qh],* "barren (woman)," in 6QEnGiants (6Q8) 1:6 (*MPAT* 19:1.6). Though Grelot prefers to render *heauton* as *garmeh,* lit. "his bone," using the Christian Palestinian substitute for the reflexive pronoun instead of the Syriac *napšeh,* the latter is now well attested in Palestinian Aramaic texts: 1QapGen 19:23 (in the feminine *npšh,* lit. "her soul," as a substitute for "herself"); Mur 18:9 (*MPAT* 39:9); 19:26 (*MPAT* 40:26); 21:21 (*MPAT* 42:21); 27:6 (*MPAT* 46:6); 28:11,12 (*MPAT* 47:11,12); pap?HevB ar 15 (*MPAT* 51:15), etc.

*waṣlēm 'ăbēd nēsab/nāsib,* "and he took/taking the form of a slave,"

*Morphē* is again rendered by Aramaic *ṣēlēm,* as in v. 6. Aramaic *'bd,* "slave," is attested in 11QtgJob 2:5 (= Hebrew 19:16); 35:7 (= 40:28); 1QapGen 22:6. Following Grelot, I have put *wĕ-* at the head of this line. Then it may be debated whether one should use the perfect *nĕsab,* "he took," or the participle *nāsib,* "taking" (for which, see Dan 5:1; 6:7; cf. BLA §811). The verb *nsb* is attested in 1QapGen 20:9,27,34; in 20:27 it renders Hebrew *'eqqah* of Gen 12:19, where the Greek of the LXX has *elabon.*

*wĕbidmût 'ĕnāš hāwē',* "and being in the likeness of a man,"

בֹ ד ١ Գ٦ 𝔳א ٦ ١

I follow Grelot in using *bidmût 'ĕnāš* and in taking the latter word as a collective singular; thus it equals *en homoiōmati anthrōpōn*. The phrase *kdmwt 'nš* occurs in 4QEn astrᵇ 26:5; cf. *BMAP* 3:21. Compare Ezek 1:5, *dĕmût 'ādām, LXX homoiōma anthrōpou*. Again I use *wĕ-* at the beginning of the line and the participle *hw'*; Grelot has used the perfect *hăwā'*, taking the participle *genomenos* as a grecism (?). See *BMAP* 4:6, where the participle *hwh* expresses contemporary time with the perfect *yhbth*.

*wĕbihzû mištĕkaḥ kĕbar-'ĕnāš,* "and being found in appearance like a son of man," ὡς ἀνθρωπος AS α mon

Greek *schēmati* has been rendered as *bihzû* by Grelot because *hăzû,* "appearance," is found in Dan 7:20 and also in 4QEn astrᵇ 26:4,5; 4QEnᵉ 4 iii [21]; 4Q'Amramᵇ 1.13,14 (*MPAT* 23:1.13,14). The LXX of Dan 7:20 uses *prosopsis,* and Theodotion, *horasis.* The passive of the root *škh* with a predicate is found in Dan 5:27 (*wĕtištĕkahat hassîr,* "and you were found wanting," where Theodotion has *heurēthē hysterousa*); cf. Dan 6:23 (LXX). Grelot writes *kigbar,* "like a man," which might do, but having used *'ĕnāš* in v. 7 for *anthrōpōn,* I consider *bar-'ĕnāš* more suitable here for the singular *anthrōpos.* (Though I use *bar-'ĕnāš,* I dissociate myself from the speculation that Lohmeyer read into this phrase.[23]) The noun *schēma* occurs in the LXX only in Isa 3:17, where it translates Hebrew *pōt,* "forehead." וN ß

*Verse 8*

*hašpēl napšēh,* "he humbled himself."

For the haphel of *špl,* "abase," see Dan 4:34; 5:19,22 (where the LXX renders it as *etapeinōsas*); 7:14; cf. 11QtgJob 34:7 (= Hebrew 40:11 [where the LXX again uses a form of *tapeinoun*]).

*wĕšāmôa' hăwā'/hāwē' 'ad môtā',* "and became/becoming obedient unto death."

Grelot has pointed out that the Greek adjective *hypēkoos* is found in the LXX of Prov 21:28 to translate Hebrew *šōmēa',* "one who hears, is obedient," and the targum of Proverbs renders it *šāmôaʿ*. Here we have no contemporary Aramaic adjective and are forced to make use of the later *qātôl*-type adjective, a type that is beginning to emerge in the language at this period. On the choice between the perfect or the participle of *hwʾ*, see the comment on v. 7.

## Verse 9

*lākēn ʾap śaggî hărîmēh ʾĕlāhāʾ*, "Therefore God also exalted him very much"

The illative conjunction *lākēn* is found in 11QtgJob 3:3, where it may be a hebraism borrowed from MT 20:2. Also possible would be *ʿal-kēn* (11QtgJob 37:8), which is also taken over from the Hebrew of 42:6; in this case the LXX makes use of *dio,* the very word used in Phil 2:9. The intensive *kai* can be rendered by *ʾap* (see Dan 6:23); but it should not be vocalized as *ʾof,* as Grelot has done, since that is a later Christian Palestinian pronunciation and does not correspond to the contemporary usage. When used as an adverb, *śaggî* usually precedes the verb (see Dan 5:9; 6:15,24; 7:28; AD 3:1; Aḥiqar 29,51; 1QapGen 20:8). The verb *hyperypsoun* is found in Theodotion of Dan 4:34 to translate the polel participle *mĕrômēm,* "extol, praise," in a verse that ends with *tapeinōsai.* Though one could use the polel here, as does Grelot, the nuance of *hyperypsoun* in Phil 2:9 has a different connotation. Hence my preference for the haphel *hărîmēh,* a form of which is found in Dan 5:19 in the sense of "exalting" (with honors) along with the haphel of *špl.*

*wîhab lēh lišmāʾ*, "and gave him the name"

The Greek verb *charizomai* may render Hebrew *nātan* in Esth 8:7, but it hard to be sure, since the Hebrew text has only one verb, whereas the Greek has two, *edōka kai echarisamēn;* otherwise *charizomai* occurs only in deuterocanonical writings. So, *faute de mieux,* Greek *echarisato* of Phil 2:9 is rendered by the simple *yĕhab* (see Dan 5:18). Because the best Greek reading in v. 9 has the definite article *to onoma* (mss. P⁴⁶, ℵ, A, B, C, 33, 1739, etc.), the definite direct object should be preceded by the Aramaic sign of the accusative, *lišmāʾ*.

*dî 'ēllā' min kōl šum,* "which is above every name"

The relative pronoun *dî* is employed to render the definite article that introduces the modifying prepositional phrase. For *'ēllā' min,* see Dan 6:3; 1QapGen 20:7; 4QEn^e 1 xxvi 20–21. For *šm,* see Dan 4:5.

*Verse 10*

*'al-dibrat dî bĕšum yēšûa',* "so that at Jesus' name"

The Greek conjunction *hina* of Phil 2:10 could be rendered simply by *dî,* as in Ezra 4:15; 6:10; 7:25; Dan 5:15 (Theodotion). But, as Grelot has remarked, *hina* is used in Dan 2:30 (Theodotion) and 4:17 (Theodotion) to translate Aramaic *'al-dibrat dî* (= MT 2:30; 4:14), "in order that" (*eo fine ut*), and it should be preferred because *dî* otherwise has so many different possible meanings. See also 11QtgJob 34:4, which thus renders the Hebrew *lĕma'an* of 40:8, where the LXX uses *hina.* For the construct form of *šm,* see Dan 4:5.

*kōl bĕrēk tikra',* "every knee should bow"

Though the noun *brk,* "knee," and the denominative verb *brk* occur in Dan 6:11 (*hû' bārēk 'al birkôhî,* which Theodotion renders as *ēn kamptōn epi gonata*), this line of the Philippians hymn alludes to the LXX of Isa 45:23d, which reads with a slight change of word order, *emoi kampsei pan gony,* "every knee shall bend to me," a literal translation of Hebrew *lî tikra' kōl-berek.* Though the verb *kr'* is as yet unattested in contemporary Aramaic, it is preserved in *Tg. Jonathan* at Isa 45:23.

*dî bišmayyā' wabĕ'ar'ā'' wĕlithôt 'ar'ā',* "of those in heaven, and on earth, and under the earth,"

As Grelot has noted, the three substantives in the genitive plural, *epouraniōn kai epigeiōn kai katachthoniōn,* being compound adjectives in Greek, are per se untranslatable in Aramaic; but the Aramaic *dî bĕ-* catches the sense of them very well. The length of the line is another matter; that aspect of it, along with the fact that it is inserted between two parts of the quotation from Isa 45:23de, makes some commentators suspect that it was not really part of the original Aramaic hymn. It will be recalled that this line in particular made Lohmeyer conclude that the hymn was originally composed in Greek. But the fact remains that it is easily retrojected into Aramaic and therefore may have been part of the original Jewish Christian hymn.

*Verse 11*

*wĕkōl liššān yitwaddê,* "and every tongue should declare"

This line of the hymn in Greek quotes the LXX of Isa 45:23e with a change of word order; the LXX has *exomologēsetai pasa glōssa,* an exact translation of Hebrew *tiššāba' kol-lāšôn.* However, the aphel/haphel of *ydy* means "praise, give thanks" in Dan 2:23; 6:11; 1QapGen 21:3. Though Grelot prefers this form (*yôdê*), I question the nuance thus conveyed. The ithpaal of *ydy,* however, is clearly attested in Mur 18:2 in the sense of "declaring," the nuance that is needed here. The aphel/haphel of *ydy* seems to be used in the same sense in 4QtgLev 2:6, but it is hard to say, because it is mostly restored, [*wyhwd*]'. Both of the lectionary forms of the Christian Palestinian Aramaic use *yštwdy,* the ithpaal form.

*dî mārê' yēšûa' mĕššîḥā',* "that Jesus Christ is Lord"

The predicate in the absolute state is given the prominent first place (see BLA §98a); see Dan 6:5 (*mĕhêman hû'*); cf. 1QapGen 20:2. The noun *mšyḥ'* might be vocalized simply as *mĕšîḥā',* as Grelot has read it, but John 4:25 uses the grecized form *messias,* with a double sigma, which suggests a secondary doubling of the *š* to preserve the full vowel in the first syllable (cf. *liššān, 'attûn,* "furnace," *'abbā',* "the father").[24]

*lîqār 'ĕlāhā' 'abbā',* "to the honor of God the Father."

For the construct *lîqār,* see Dan 4:27,33. Instead of the construct, Grelot uses the suffixal form *lîqārēh dî 'ĕlāhā',* which is certainly possible. But one should recall that the construct state is still fully viable at this period of Western Aramaic. From the foregoing one can see that it is not difficult to retrovert the Greek hymn of Phil 2:6-11 into a tolerable form of contemporary Western Aramaic. Grelot's effort was a step in the right direction, and it is hoped that the above attempt has been a refinement of his work. True, there are still some words that had to be invoked from Late Aramaic (*šĕlāl* for *harpagmon, šāmôaʿ* for *hypēkoos,* and *krʿ* for *kampsē*), but the vast majority of the text finds counterparts in contemporary Middle Western Aramaic.

The following form of my retroversion will permit the reader to see the Aramaic "original" as a whole:

6 *hûʾ bişlēm ʾĕlāhāʾ ʾîtôhî*
   *wĕlāʾ hăšab šĕlāl*
   *lĕmihwêʾ šāwê lēʾlāhāʾ*
7 *bĕram ʾăšad napšēh*
   *waşlēm ʿăbēd nēsab/nāsib*
   *wĕbidmût ʾĕnāš hāwēʾ*
   *wĕbihzû mištĕkah kĕbar-ʾĕnāš*
8 *hašpēl napšēh*
   *wĕšāmôaʿ hăwāʾ/hāwēʾ ʿad môtāʾ.*

9 *lākēn ʾap śaggî hărîmēh ʾĕlāhāʾ*
   *wîhab lēh lišmāʾ*
   *dî ʿēllāʾ min kōl šum*
10 *ʿal-dibrat dî bĕšum yēšûaʿ*
   *kōl bĕrēk tikraʿ*
   *dî bišmayyāʾ wabĕʾarʿāʾ wĕlithôt-ʾarʿāʾ*
11 *wēkōl liššān yitwaddê*
   *dî mārêʾ yēšûaʿ meššîhāʾ*
   *liqār ʾĕlāhāʾ ʾabbāʾ.*

## II. The Structure of Philippians 2:6–11

If one can retrovert the eighteen lines of the hymn into a form of contemporary Aramaic, there is still the question whether one can detect in it a regular pattern of accents or a fixed structure. In note 2 above I mentioned the attempts of A. Deissmann, H. Lietzmann, and M. Dibelius to set out something of the structure of the passage, the persons to whom Lohmeyer himself had referred. One of Lohmeyer's notable contributions to the study of Phil 2:6–11 was to set forth the hymn in two strophes of three verses each (vv. 6–8 and 9–11). Key to the division of the passage into strophes and verses was the three-beat line. When Lowther Clarke hailed this analysis of the passage and presented Levertoff's retroversion of the hymn into alleged Galilean Aramaic, he sensed the problem in the analysis. He wrote:

> The theory works all right until V. and VI. [= vv. 10 and 11]. I.–IV. are in hymn form, but V., VI. are obviously St. Paul's own application of Isa. xlv.23 to Jesus. In VI. the beats appear to be correct, but do not possess the correct rhythm on recitation.[25]

This was, however, more of a critique of Levertoff's retroversion than it was of Lohmeyer's analysis of the Greek. I have already mentioned above the fact that Levertoff sometimes accented reduced vowels to get his beats. But the problem is more acute.

Grelot proposed an entirely new structure of the hymn, based more on similarity of forms in the Greek text itself. Then he proposed to translate that structure into Aramaic, and the result is amorphous. Though he retains many of the lines of the Lohmeyer analysis, he has rearranged them in four sections, and it is indeed difficult to perceive the rationale behind them.

Part of the problem is that the lines, though for the most part of equal length and of three components, are not all such. W. Michaelis spotted the problem.[26] Whether in Greek or in Aramaic, the first part of v. 8 has merely two words (*etapeinōsen heauton; hašpēl napšēh*); and the first part of v. 9 must have more than three beats (*dio kai ho theos hyperypsōsen auton; lākēn śaggî' hărîmēh 'ĕlāhā'*).

Martin, though he recognized that Lohmeyer's analysis had the "least difficulty," decided to eliminate vv. 8c (*thanatou de staurou*), 10c (*epouraniōn kai epigeiōn kai katachthoniōn*), and 11c (*eis doxan theou patros*). Moreover, he proposed to see in the rest "a series of couplets, in six pairs . . . arranged in such a way that they could have been chanted in an antiphonal manner."[27] But once again the couplets turn out to be of unequal length. Thus to Aa, (*hos*) *en morphē theou hyparchōn,* must correspond Ab, *ouch harpagmon hēgēsato to einai isa theō,* a clause that is too long.

Because there is such a problem in this matter of accents, compound words, and the structure of the hymn, whether in Greek or in Aramaic, I have preferred to remain with the basic suggestion of Lohmeyer and propose the hymn as a composition of eighteen simple lines, which can be further divided into the two strophes of three groups of three-lined verses — provided one recognizes that it is not possible to arrive at a perfect pattern of three beats to a line.

If this attempt to retrovert Phil 2:6–11 into a form of contemporary Aramaic is seen to be valid, it will at least support the contention that the passage represents a pre-Pauline rhetorical composition of Jewish-Christian origin.

### III. Meaning and Purpose of the Hymn

Paul has thus taken over from a contemporary Jewish Christian liturgy a hymn to Christ, which makes six christological affirmations. Each group of three-lined verses in the two strophes declares something about Christ Jesus. The two strophes would describe a parabola-like structure, the first arm of which would depict the descent and the second the ascent movement. In the first strophe the first group of three-liners treats of Jesus' divine preexistence, the second of the humiliation of his incarnation, the third of the further humiliation of his death (to which Paul himself would have added, "even death upon a cross!"). In the second strophe the first group of three-liners describes his celestial exaltation, the second the adoration of him by the universe, and the third Jesus' new name, *Kyrios.* To bring out the meaning of the six groups of three-liners, the following translation of the hymn may suffice:

6 Who, though of divine status,
    did not treat like a miser's booty
    his right to be like God,
7 but emptied himself of it,
    to take up the status of a slave
    and become like human beings;
    having assumed human form,
8 he still further humbled himself

with an obedience that meant death —
    even death upon a cross!

9 That is why God has so greatly exalted him
    and given him the name,
    which is above all others:
10 that everyone at Jesus' name
    should bend his knee
    in heaven, on earth, and under the earth!
11 that every tongue should declare
    unto the glory of God the Father
    that Jesus Christ is Lord!

Thus this early Jewish Christian Aramaic hymn serves to extol the glorious name that Paul uses for the risen Christ, "Lord," giving poetic utterance to the basic Christian confession and proclamation, "Jesus is Lord!" (1 Cor 12:3; Rom 10:9). It is thus a rare Pauline text that speaks of the preexistence of the son and acknowledges "his right to be like God" (v. 6), making understandable how Paul may well call Christ Jesus even *theos*, "God" (Rom 9:5).[28] For, after all, he affirms in using this hymn that he regards Christ Jesus as worthy of the same adoration that Isa 45:23 accorded to Yahweh in the Old Testament. Even though we admit that Paul himself did not compose this Aramaic hymn, he has at least made use of it in Greek form and thus incorporated it into his way of thinking.

Noteworthy is the Greek addition that he makes to v. 8, "even death upon a cross!" This addition stresses the death of Jesus, giving an emphasis that appears elsewhere in his letters to the theology of the cross. See, e.g., Rom 4:25; 1 Cor 1:18. For Paul maintained that he preached "Christ crucified" (1 Cor 1:23) and insisted with the Galatians that he depicted for them "Jesus Christ publicly portrayed as crucified" (Gal 3:1).[29] So one is not suprised at the addition that is made in v. 8 of this adopted hymn.

In the immediate hortatory context of the letter to the Philippians, this hymn to Christ as Kyrios thus recalls for his readers the example of the historical Jesus, who according to this hymnic confession of the early Jewish Christian church has become the model of Christian conduct. Though he possessed divine equality and its consequent privilege to appear like Yahweh in glory, he did not stand on this dignity. He poured himself out for the sake of humanity, humbling himself to become a human being and share human status and further humbling himself in dying as a crucified criminal. Such a model is proposed to the Philippians, and to Christians of all ages. It is a distinctive pattern of Christian life that no other New Testament writer has so forcefully proposed.[30]

# CHAPTER EIGHT

# Paul and Preaching

We realize today that in dealing with Paul the Apostle, we are dealing with one of the great preachers of the Christian church. What he accomplished for the Christian movement, he accomplished through preaching, through proclaiming "God's gospel," as he himself called it (Rom 1:1). He has thus become the perennial example par excellence for Christian preachers and evangelizers of all ages. But the problem is that what he preached is not what preachers of today often do. For he preached "Christ crucified" (1 Cor 1:23) and announced "the story of the cross" (1 Cor 1:18). And though he claimed that he did not do it with great eloquence, yet he realized that God himself "chose what is foolish in the world to shame the wise, chose what is weak in the world to shame the strong" (1 Cor 1:27).

There are two aspects of the topic, Paul and preaching, that should be considered and they may form the heads under which I shall discuss the question: (I) Paul's own awareness of apostolic preaching; and (II) how one might preach on Pauline theological topics.

## I. Paul's Own Awareness of Apostolic Preaching

Paul's awareness of his role as an apostolic preacher shines through many passages in his writings. Even if his heritage comes to us in the form of letters, and it has had great influence on later Christian writers who imitated his epistolary practice, Paul never boasts of having been called by God to write letters to Christian communities. He is rather aware of having been (1) called as an apostle, (2) sent to preach the gospel, especially to the Gentiles, and (3) sent to preach the gospel of Christ Jesus crucified and raised by the Father in order to elicit faith from human beings.

(1) Paul's apostolic role was apparently challenged in the early church in some quarters. Yet he stoutly defended his commission, "Am I not an apostle? Have I not seen Jesus our Lord? . . . If to others I am not an apostle, to you at least I am" (1 Cor 9:1-2). In Galatians he explains how he has "seen" the risen Lord: God himself had accorded him a revelation of "his Son" (1:16); hence his commission was "not from human beings or through a human being, but through Jesus Christ and God the Father who raised him from the dead" (1:1). In Paul's eyes that commission put him on a par with "those who were apostles before me" (Gal 1:17), even though he was keenly aware that the risen Christ had appeared to him "last of all, as to one untimely born" (1 Cor 15:8). Because of that revelation he rightly considered himself to be "called to be an apostle" (Rom 1:1), even though he also admitted that he was "the least of the apostles, unworthy to be called an apostle" because he had "persecuted the church of God"—yet "by God's grace I am what I am, and his grace toward me has not been in vain" (1 Cor 15:9-10). (2) Paul was aware that he had been called to preach the gospel, especially to the Gentiles. He insisted,

> I thank God that I baptized none of you except Crispus and Gaius, lest anyone might claim that you were baptized in my name. (I did baptize the household of Stephanas too—but I am not aware of having baptized anyone else.) For Christ did not send me to baptize, but to preach the gospel, not with eloquent wisdom, lest the cross of Christ be emptied of its meaning (1 Cor 1:14-17).

In the passage where this statement occurs Paul has been arguing against the factions that divided the church of Corinth; and strangely enough, he puts more emphasis on preaching than on baptizing. To many modern preachers the former would seem to be oriented to the latter, and the latter more important. Yet Paul insisted that he had been called to *preach*. In Gal 1:15-16 he adds, "When it pleased God, who had set me apart from my mother's womb and had called me with his grace, to reveal his Son to me, that I might preach him among the Gentiles, I did not confer with flesh and blood," i.e. with other human beings. For he realized that his experience near Damascus had given him an insight into the mystery of Christ that no human being's information about Christ could surpass. It was not a cinematic reproduction of the ministry of Jesus of Nazareth, but an understanding of the meaning of Christ Jesus for humanity. That is why Paul's writings create an anomaly for us Christians of later generations. For in God's providence what was first recorded in writing, in the scriptural heritage of the Christian church, was not an account of what Jesus did and said, but the Pauline interpretation of the significance of what his ministry, death, and resurrection meant for humanity. This comes to us above all in the letters of Paul, as he sought to cope with problems in the churches that he had founded or to sum up aspects of his understanding of the gospel of Jesus Christ (especially in the Epistle to the Romans). What Paul preached, then, and summarized in his epistolary instructions and teachings are what we have inherited from the first great Christian theologian. What Paul recorded in these letters he had first preached and proclaimed. The proclaimed word preceded the written word.

(3) Paul was also aware that he was to preach the gospel of Christ crucified, dead, and raised, as a means of eliciting faith from human beings. He had to preach (a) *Christ crucified*. "We preach indeed Christ crucified, to Jews a stumbling block and to Gentiles foolishness, but to those who are called, whether Jews or Greeks, Christ the power of God and the wisdom of God" (1 Cor 1:23-26). (b) *God's gospel*. He was called to preach "the gospel of God" (Rom 1:1), i.e. the good news that comes from God"; "the gospel of Jesus Christ" (Gal 1:7), i.e. the good news about Jesus Christ and salvation, or even the good news that comes through him. (c) *The faith*. For it was reported of him that "he who once persecuted us is now preaching the faith that he once tried to destroy" (Gal 1:23).

For Paul *euangelion* denoted the activity of evangelization, but also the content of his apostolic message: what he preached and proclaimed. His gospel was revelatory or apocalyptic (making known God's new way of bringing salvation to humanity, Rom 1:17); it was dynamic (unleashing a new salvific force [*dynamis*] into human history, Rom 1:16); it was kerygmatic (proclaiming God's new mode of salvation through the death and resurrection of Christ Jesus, 1 Cor 15:1–7); but it was also normative (standing critically over Christian conduct, and even that of church officials [because it enabled Paul to confront Peter publicly when he was not walking according to the truth of the gospel, Gal 2:11–14]); and promissory (bringing to fulfillment the promises made by God long ago through the patriarchs and the prophets of old, Rom 1:2). For such reasons Paul could boast that he was not ashamed of the gospel.

What underlies such a conviction is the understanding of Christian faith itself. The root of Paul's proclaimed faith is "the word of Christ," i.e. the word about Christ and the word that stems from Christ. The human being accosted by that word must respond in faith: this is "the word of faith that we preach" (Rom 10:8). The response of one so accosted is double: "If you confess with your lips that Jesus is Lord and believe in your hearts that God raised him from the dead, you will be saved" (Rom 10:9). This the Pauline summation of faith. It begins with the proclamation of "the word of Christ" and with a corresponding assent to the lordship of Christ, "Jesus is Lord" (see also 1 Cor 12:3), the object of Paul's kerygmatic preaching. But the response to that proclamation was not merely faith as the result of hearing (*pistis ex akoēs*), i.e. an assent of lips and heart to the proposition that "Jesus is Lord." Though it had to begin with such an assent to a proposition, it eventually had to lead to the dedication of the whole person to God in Christ Jesus; it had to involve *hypakoē pisteōs,* "a commitment of faith" (Rom 1:5). Hence Paul was able to write to the Philippians, "Let your manner of life be worthy of the gospel of Christ, so that whether I come and see you or am absent, I may hear of you that you stand firm in one spirit, with one mind striving side by side for the faith of the gospel . . ." (1:27).

But Paul was also aware that such a commitment of faith had to come from the preached word of commissioned, apostolic preachers. "How are they to believe in him about whom they have never heard? How are they to hear [about him] without a preacher? And how may they preach unless they have been sent? (Rom 10:14b-15). Clearly, for Paul the genuine "preached word" is brought to human beings, Jews and Greeks alike, only by commissioned, apostolic preachers. Such was the awareness of Paul about his apostolic role as a preacher of the gospel of Jesus Christ, the risen Lord.[1]

## II. How to Preach on Pauline Topics

I have to begin my discussion of this matter with a quotation from the latest book of the New Testament. By the time that 2 Peter was composed (toward the beginning of the second century A.D.), Paul's letters had apparently already been gathered into a corpus and were being read widely in ecclesial communities of the time. Then, too, Pauline teachings were beginning to create a problem in the early church, and the author felt obliged to warn his readers thus:

> Consider the longsuffering of the Lord as salvation. So too our beloved brother Paul wrote to you according to the wisdom granted to him, speaking of this as he does in all his letters. Some things in them are hard to understand, which the unlearned and unstable twist to their own destruction, as they do the other Scriptures (2 Pet 3:15-16).

Any advice in the twentieth century to preachers on Pauline letters must begin with the caution expressed by the author of 2 Peter: "Some things in them are hard to understand."

And yet that is why the preacher in the twentieth century has been commissioned, i.e. ordained. Pauline topics are just as much part of the written word of God as the sayings and parables of Jesus in the gospel tradition. This means that the commissioned preacher must, first of all, study the Pauline letters and master the Pauline topics. For some reason, in God's providence the earliest writings of the New Testament were not the narrative accounts of what Jesus did and said, but the interpretation of what he achieved for humanity, the Pauline interpretation of the Christ-event, as difficult as that interpretation may prove to be. Moreover, one must recall that the

Pauline interpretation of the Christ-event, of Christ Jesus and his ministry, death, and resurrection, has been the springboard for most of the dogmatic tradition of the Catholic church. More than any other New Testament writer Paul's formulations have influenced the Christian teaching of the patristic, medieval, reformation, and modern periods.

In this regard, it might be well to mention that at the time of the Reformation Christian preaching was normally at a nadir and Pauline topics were generally neglected. The emphasis that Luther and Zwingli put on the "preached word" was wholly derived from Paul (Rom 10:8, "the word of faith that we preach"). The mode of preaching inherited from the medieval Spirituals had dwindled into pious story-telling, and Zwingli stood up in Catholic churches to interrupt such "sermonizing" to challenge the friars that they were neglecting the Word of God, the gospel, especially the Pauline gospel. The tremendous heritage of the "preached word" had slipped into desuetude, and it was gradually recovered in the Reformation and the Counter-Reformation by the emphasis on the preached word and a return to Pauline topics.

But how does one recapture that genuine Christian tradition of preaching the word of faith, of preaching on the significance of the Christ-event, as Paul of Tarsus saw it?

(Before I try to answer that question, I have to digress for a moment, to say something about a problem that the lectionary often creates, especially for the Sunday liturgies. How often have we encountered selections in the lectionary from the Old Testament, from Paul, and from a Gospel that do not hang together, that have no thread that joins them? When there is such a joining thread, it is easy enough to comment on the meaning of all three passages, and adopt the common element as the topic for the homily.

In the present three-year lectionary for Sundays, selections for Year A include passages from 1 Corinthians 1–4, Romans (16 Sundays), Philippians, and 1 Thessalonians; selections for Year B include passages from 1 Corinthians 6–11, 2 Corinthians (eight Sundays), and Ephesians; and selections for Year C include selections from 1 Corinthians 12–15, 2 Corinthians, Galatians, Colossians, Philemon, 1–2 Timothy, and 2 Thessalonians. Thus most of the Pauline corpus is represented, and

Titus turns up in Christmas liturgies. Still other passages occur in the two-year week-day lectionary, not to mention selections in the feast-day liturgies, the proper of the saints, and votive masses.

Though the Pauline corpus is thus represented, the problem is often that the selection from Paul is a snippet. Again, though in the Sunday liturgies there is frequently enough a harmonization of the Old Testament passage and the Gospel, the Pauline passage is just "there," without any real connection with the other two selections. Moreover, many of the Pauline selections are drawn from the hortatory parts of his letters, avoiding the more difficult doctrinal or didactic passages.

When one preaches, then, on the Old Testament and the Gospel, there is no need to try to bring in the Pauline passage. For that would be to harmonize what is not meant to be harmonized. If, however, one decides to preach on the Pauline passage, then there is no need to bring in details from the other two.[2]

To try to answer the question posed above, how to preach on the significance of the Christ-event, as Paul saw it, I shall make comments of two sorts, first, of a generic, abstract sort, and then, second, by way of example.

*First,* some generic advice. (a) One has to realize that the Pauline interpretation of the Christ-event is part of the word of God. To preach the word of God is to apply that word and its meaning to particular twentieth-century congregations, who are not the same as the audience for whom Paul himself wrote his letters. The preacher must realize that he is not just reading a piece of secular literature to his congregation. Literary though the Pauline writing might on occasion be, it is still the word of God, the means chosen by God and inspired by his Spirit to express his presence to Christians of all ages. This aspect of the Pauline text must be grasped by the preacher himself and introduced into the very liturgy of which the homily or sermon is a vital part.

To preach the word of God is to interpret it, and the preacher thus has to become a commentator or interpreter of the Pauline text. To preach from the Pauline writings, one has to explain its meaning, fashioning that explanation into a homily or sermon, and making the necessary application of the Pauline message to the congregation assembled for the liturgy in which the homily or sermon is presented.

(b) One has, therefore, to study the Pauline letters in order to comprehend their essential teaching. It is not sufficient to read a passage from one of Paul's letters in the lectionary and use it as a springboard for extraneous comments on a phrase or verse in it. Rather, the preacher has to learn to immerse himself in the message of the Pauline letter being used; he has to learn what the letter *as a whole* is all about. In the homily he should, therefore, in a sentence or two situate for his audience the place that the passage holds in a given letter, explain the context of Paul's remarks, and sum up the meaning of them. The immediate context of the passage is important. For instance, in Year C, on the Second Sunday, 1 Cor 12:4-11 (about the gifts of the Spirit) is read. Yet that passage is only a part of chaps. 12-14, which deal with varied spiritual gifts, their place in the body of Christ, and the dangers from esteeming some of them (e.g. the gift of tongues) too highly. Readings for three Sundays are taken from these chapters, and the organization of the homilies may be problematic as a result. But if the context has been explained, then the reading that the congregation has just listened to should become more intelligible to them.

(c) To preach well on a Pauline topic, one has to understand something about Pauline theology itself. Paul himself has written letters, which were often devoted to disparate, *ad hoc* problems, and he has nowhere presented us with a synthesis of his teaching. The closest one comes to such a synthesis is Romans, the most difficult of his letters.

Though Philip Melanchthon regarded Romans as a "summary of all Christian doctrine,"[3] we realize today that it cannot be so characterized, for it is not even a compendium of all Pauline doctrine. It lacks any discussion of Paul's views on the church or the Eucharist and is almost devoid of eschatological teaching. Paul wrote that important letter, first of all, to introduce himself to the church of the Christians of Rome, the capital of the empire, which he himself had not founded, and secondly, to present to those Christians an exposé of what he understood as the significance of the gospel of Christ Jesus in a summation of his missionary reflections on that gospel that he had been preaching for years in the eastern Mediterranean world. In it he sets forth his thoughts about the gospel of salvation for Jew and Greek alike, about the gospel of justification by grace through faith, about the gospel of God's love poured into human hearts through the holy Spirit which has been given to them, and about the gospel's relation to the people of Israel.

Again, Ephesians is likewise a synthesis of Pauline teaching, echoing many things that are found in the uncontested letters of Paul, but it is Deutero-Pauline, composed by a disciple of Paul, who insists on the unity or unicity of the church, in a way that Paul himself never did in his own letters. A good example of how Pauline teaching (about justification by faith) is reworked in Ephesians can be found in 2:8–10. Here all the characteristic terminology associated with justification is now related to salvation:

> "By grace you have been *saved* through faith; and this is not of your own doing, but it is a gift of God—not because of deeds, lest anyone begin to boast. For we are his workmanship, created in Christ Jesus for good deeds, which God prepared in advance that we might walk in them."

Today we understand Pauline theology as the synthetic summary of Paul's teaching. The preacher has to understand something about Pauline theology as a whole—the theology of his uncontested letters, the theology of the Deutero-Pauline letters, and the theology of the Pastoral letters—in order to comprehend the teaching of a given passage of the Pauline corpus. Yet the preacher has also to remember that Pauline theology is like the icing on the cake; it is the part that we all want to have, to partake of, and know something about. Yet it is something that we do not get unless we have the cake itself, and that means, in terms of Scripture, the exegetical study of the passages wherein the individual Pauline topic is enshrined. Such exegetical study is needed to prepare the preacher for his homily. It is not meant that the homily itself would be exegetical—at least in most ordinary cases. It may have to be such on occasion, when a difficult passage is presented in the lectionary, a passage that puzzles the people who listen to it or a passage that just cries out for explanation. Then the homilist has to situate the passage in its proper context in the letter and explain its essential message. He has to comment on the difficult phrases or words that are in the passage.

(d) Part of Pauline theology deals with the effects of the Christ-event, ten of which can be singled out: Justification, Salvation, Reconciliation, Expiation, Redemption, Freedom, Sanctification, Transformation, New Creation, and Glorification.[4]

Some of these terms are no longer part of twentieth-century parlance, which creates a problem in preaching on them. People today do not know what "justification" means, and yet that effect of the Christ-event takes pride of place among the ten. It is the cardinal effect of the Christ-event in the most important letters of Paul, the one of which Luther made so much. Justification by grace through faith was the answer to the cry of his conscience, "How do I get a gracious God?"

And yet, when the Lutheran World Federation met in Helsinki in 1963 on the topic of Justification by Faith, the delegates could no longer agree or find a common understanding about the topic. They had to admit in the opening paragraph of their report that this was no longer a concern of modern people in the twentieth century: how one finds a gracious God. The concern is rather, How do I find meaning in life?[5] Yet the delegates to the congress eventually realized that "finding meaning in life" is only another way of putting "justification by grace through faith."

Again, the National Dialogue of Lutherans and Roman Catholics recently took up this basic topic, and after years of discussion came out with a common statement on it, which was issued to the press on a Sunday evening with an embargo until the following Friday. That evening Dan Rather announced on his CBS nightly news that a group of Lutheran and Catholic theologians had come to an agreement about "*Salvation* by Faith*," and missed the whole point of the common statement. Why? Because "justification" would have been unintelligible to most of his hearers. Rather did for his listeners what the epistle to the Ephesians had already done for its readers.

What, then, is the preacher today to do with such a topic if it occurs in the reading of the liturgy? The answer is that he *must explain it;* he may not avoid it. This is one of those difficult Pauline topics that needs exegetical comment. Yet he must not only explain it, but also paraphrase it and make it

intelligible in twentieth-century parlance. After all, it is a crucial
Pauline topic, at the heart of Pauline teaching. If one is going
to preach on Paul, one cannot avoid it. Moreover, in the
litigious world in which we live this judicial way in which Paul
has described an effect of the Christ-event would not be that
strange to twentieth-century Christians, when it is properly
understood and explained. They know what it means to appear
before a judge in a law court. They can understand how their
sins and the evil they do make it necessary that they one day
appear before the divine tribunal (Rom 2:5-10; 2 Cor 5:10).
But what they do not realize is the Pauline solution to that
critical appearance: that Christ Jesus, by his passion, death,
and resurrection, has brought it about that they may appear
before that tribunal as acquitted and declared innocent, in fact
justified by the grace of God through the Spirit of Christ, which
has been poured into Christians hearts.

(e) But there are many other, less complicated Pauline topics
that lend themselves to easier exposé. Among these would be
other effects of the Christ-event mentioned earlier. Many are
the topics about the influence of the Spirit in our lives, about
the role of the church as the body of Christ, and counsels about
the conduct of Christian life. No matter what the Pauline topic
is, it usually calls for some explanation. Homilies devoted to
Pauline topics, even the easier topics, should be expository or
explanatory, since Pauline terminology is not obvious. Hence,
the modern preacher who would preach on Pauline topics has
to realize that most of the homily will be expository, instruct-
ing God's people, who are so hungry for a greater comprehension of the written word of God. They have read and listened
to Paul's letters; so the preacher has the obligation to explain
the things in them "that are hard to understand," as 2 Peter
noted about "the letters of our beloved brother Paul."

Even in relatively simple Pauline passages there are terms
that the Apostle uses that would be unfamiliar to modern
readers, "flesh" and "spirit," or "spirit" and "letter," or
"parousia." "Flesh" is not merely something related to sex; and
the "spirit" might be understood as "the holy Spirit," but also
as the human "spirit."

Again, Paul often quotes the Old Testament to bolster up
his point, but without explaining the pertinence of it. In this

case, the preacher has to explain not only the Pauline context and use of the Old Testament, but even the context of the Old Testament passage that is being quoted.

Moreover, one would have to explain that some Pauline passages are time-conditioned, e.g. some of his views on women. That difficult passage on wives as subject to their husbands in Eph 5:21–33 would call for particular explanation.[6]

(f) The Pauline corpus in the New Testament is itself a problem, since only seven of the thirteen letters are normally recognized as authentic: 1 Thessalonians, Galatians, Philippians, 1–2 Corinthians, Romans, and Philemon. Some are regarded today as Deutero-Pauline, i.e. written by a disciple of Paul: Colossians, Ephesians, and 2 Thessalonians. Finally, the Pastorals (Titus, 1–2 Timothy) are often described as pseudepigraphic. This means that the one who would preach on the Deutero-Paulines or the Pastorals would have to phrase carefully what he says about such writings in the Pauline corpus. After all, there are many lay Catholics who have had college courses on the Bible or the New Testament and would be aware of such distinctions, and might wonder whether the preacher himself were aware of them. This would be particularly acute when one is preaching on the ecclesiology of Colossians and Ephesians — in passages that do occur at times in the Sunday lectionary selections.

*Second,* some examples of Pauline homiletic treatment. (a) If one were to preach on a Pauline letter as a whole, one should then indicate the occasion for the letter (and possibly whether there be any similarity between the preacher's congregation and the one to which Paul writes). If the letter were 1 Thessalonians, the preacher should indicate the problem that faced Paul as he wrote: whether the risen Christ had power over those who had passed on from this life, whether they too would share in the destiny promised to those who might still be alive at the coming of the Lord. Modern people might not have the concern that the Thessalonians did about their already deceased confrères, but they are concerned about the afterlife. Paul's message in 1 Thess 4:13–18 about the destiny of the Christian "to be always with the Lord" would then be a consolation even to twentieth-century Christians.

But the preacher would have to distinguish the genuine

Pauline message (about the Christian destiny: "to be always with the Lord") from the apocalyptic stageprops that Paul has used to describe the parousia (stage-props such as the descent of the Lord from heaven, the cry of command, the archangel's call, the sound of God's trumpet, the rapture, the clouds). Obviously, Paul knows nothing about how the parousia will take place; he adopts, therefore, elements from apocalyptic writing to describe such an event. The stageprops are not part of the essential message of the passage. This is a good example of how the modern preacher would have to explain to his audience the real sense of the Pauline letter and demythologize the apocalyptic elements. It would also mean that the preacher would be able to interpret the passage properly so that the listeners do not come away with a fundamentalist conviction about the final "rapture," which Bible Belt preachers like to proclaim. Yet that means that the preacher would have to know what 1 Thessalonians 4 is all about.

(b) If one were preaching on deuterocanonical Eph 5:21-33, that important passage on married life that causes so many problems for modern wives, one would have to make several important distinctions. (i) The preacher would indicate that this instruction is part of a larger section in the hortatory part of Ephesians, 5:21 to 6:9, a section in which the author has incorporated what Luther in his translation of the Bible into German called a *Haustafel,* a list of domestic duties. It gives instructions for the proper conduct of Christian husbands and wives (5:21-33), for parents and children (6:1-4), and for slaves and masters (6:5-9). (ii) The preacher would stress the *mutual obligation* of both husband and wife. The passage always sounds derogatory of women, because it suggests, "Wives, be subject to your husbands, as to the Lord" (5:22). Modern women, hearing that in church liturgies, tend to be offended because it seems to say that they are inferior. Yet inferiority is never expressed in that passage. In fact, it begins explicitly, "Be subject to one another out of reverence for Christ" (5:21). The main point in the insistence on subjection is the *mutual obligation* of husband and wife to one another. If it says that the wife should be submissive, that does not mean that she should consider herself "inferior" to her husband. In the same passage the husband is also instructed, "Husbands, love your wives, as Christ loved the church and gave himself up for her" (5:25). (iii) The preacher would have to cope with the time-conditioned element in the passage, the social status of women. Yet the author of the passage is emphasizing an important element in the marital union. The wife and husband as female and male members of the human race who join in marriage for the love of one another are different from each other; they are psychologically disposed in different ways to be complements to each other. The author of this passage tries to reckon with this difference, but he stresses the difference in the time-conditioned sociological way characteristic of his day, by insisting that the wife should be subject to her husband, even as he likewise insists that the husband should love his wife. The modern social status of a wife in marriage has changed, but there is still a perennial teaching in this passage that must be respected in any modern marriage: the mutual obligation of the spouses to each other even in a household where the husband is regarded as the paterfamilias. (iv) The preacher would have to exploit the meaning of the Genesis text that is quoted in 5:31, and its hidden meaning. For the author not only quotes the Old Testament, but comments on it in a manner very similar to the Essene/Qumran mode of commenting on Scripture in the pesharim (commentaries) on Old Testament writings: "This mystery is a profound one," and the mystery means the hidden sense of Gen 2:24, "For this reason a man shall leave his father and mother and be joined to his wife, and the two shall become one flesh." For that verse of Genesis is not merely a reference to marriage, stressing the marital union of man and woman, of which it speaks on the surface, but also to the relationship between Christ and his church, which is the symbolic and fuller sense of the Genesis passage. This symbolic sense also has to be exploited in the homily, for it brings out the sublime meaning of marriage as an image of the relation of the church to Christ.

(c) Finally, let us take the readings from the twenty-third Sunday of the year: Ezek 33:7–9; Rom 13:8–10; and Matt 18:15–20. Both the Old Testament passage and the Gospel deal with fraternal correction, but the passage from Romans is only in the most remote way related to it. It is a good example of a set of readings, in which the preacher might well choose to preach on the Pauline passage alone. If he were to do so, then the following points might be considered. Since the passage from Romans is a good example of a snippet, I cite it as a whole:

> Owe no one a debt, save that of loving one another; for the one who loves his neighbor has fulfilled the law. The commandment, 'You shall not commit adultery, You shall not kill, You shall not steal, You shall not covet' — or any commandment — are summed up in this one, 'You shall love your neighbor as yourself.' Love does no wrong to a neighbor, for love is the fulfillment of the law (13:8–10).

(i) The preacher should indicate that the passage comes from the hortatory section of Paul's letter to the Romans, wherein the Apostle is explaining that Spirit-guided Christian life must be worship paid to God. A detail in that exhortation is how Christian love of the neighbor is part of that life of worship. That supplies the context in which the Pauline instruction is given.

(ii) The essential teaching is that love fulfills the law: what the law expected of human beings of old is now fulfilled by the love of one's neighbor. Paul is saying that the Christian whose faith works itself out through love (Gal 5:6) is, in effect, fulfilling all the demands that the law once made of Israel of old. Paul means, then, that the Christian has no real need of the law as a norm of conduct because the one who expresses love toward one's neighbor is in fact conducting himself or herself according to the demands of the law.

(iii) Though Paul cites the Decalogue (Deut 5:17–20; Exod 20:13–17) as an example of the law to be observed, his real Old Testament citation proves his point, "You shall love your neighbor as yourself" (Lev 19:18b). Thus Paul uses the Old Testament itself to show that love is a major factor in Christian life. The Christian who loves and so lives in faith and love fulfills God's law and thus pays homage to him who is the author of it. In this way the love of a Christian is worship paid to God, the goal of Christian conduct — the theme of the hortatory section of Romans.

(iv) Three minor points might be added: (aa) the strange oxymoron that Paul uses to introduce the teaching about the role of love. "Owe no one a debt save that of loving one another" (13:8). It is strange because one may ask, How can Paul speak of love as a "debt," when by nature love is something that is freely given; it is not "owed" to anyone. (bb) The love of which Paul speaks is the love of the neighbor; nothing is said about the love of God, which might be thought to be more appropriate in Christian life lived as worship of God. Paul stresses here in the hortatory section of Romans the love of neighbor because earlier in the doctrinal section of Romans, in 8:28, he has already said, "We realize that all things work together for the good of those who love God." It is not that Paul is remiss in not insisting on the love of God; he has already treated that, but in this hortatory section, when he is exhorting the Christians of Rome to live their lives as an act of worship, he can think of no better fulfillment of that which God demands of them than that they should love their neighbors. (cc) It might be explained that in Lev 19:18b, which Paul cites in order to sum up the law, the love of neighbor expressed there is the love of one's fellow Jew, because v. 18a begins, "You shall not take vengeance or bear a grudge against the children of your own people." Thus the "neighbor" of v. 18b is one of the "children of your own people." In the Pauline context, however, the meaning would have a larger extension, since he has often spoken in Romans of both Jews and Gentiles, barbarians and Greeks.

Now such elements as I have outlined above occupy a little less than fifty lines. This succinct statement could easily be built into a fifteen or twenty minute homily by the preacher who would dress it up in his own style and make the proper applications to the modern scene. These would not be difficult because there is always room for a good homily on the love of one's neighbor. In this case, it would be necessary to stress how Paul the Apostle, writing to a community that he himself did not found, was moved to exhort them to such a basic demand of Christian life. In doing so, he did not hesitate to call upon a fundamental teaching of the Pentateuch itself. What is stated there, however, gets across the basic message in the Pauline passage selected for use in the liturgical cycle.[7]

# Notes

## Notes to Chapter 1

1. Cf. Acts 13:21. See further H. Dessau, "Der Name des Apostels Paulus," *Hermes* 45 (1910) 347–68; G. H. Harrer, "Saul Who Is Also Called Paul," *HTR* 33 (1940) 19–33.

2. See "Paulus," *Der kleine Pauly: Lexikon der Antike* (5 vols.; ed. K. Ziegler and W. Sontheimer; Munich: A. Druckenmüller, 1964–75) 4. 562–68; *The Oxford Classical Dictionary* (2d ed.; ed. N. G. L. Hammond and N. H. Scullard; Oxford: Clarendon, 1976) 791–92.

3. See also Acts 16:37–38, and the indirect references in Acts 25:9–12; 26:31–32; 28:17–19. Though W. Stegemann ("War der Apostel Paulus ein römischer Bürger?" *ZNW* 78 [1987] 200–29) feels that a consideration of what is known of the socio-historical conditions of Tarsus and of the granting of citizenship to people in the Roman empire of the time, and especially to Jews, makes it unlikely that Paul would have been a Roman citizen, the last word has not been written on this topic. After all, there is no reason that Paul should mention his Roman citizenship in any of his letters, not even in the Letter to the Romans. What he writes of there has no real relationship to himself being a citizen of the Roman empire, not even what he says of the Christian relations to governing authorities in Rom 13:1–7. That may reflect the fact that he is writing to the Christians of the capital of the empire, as some commentators hold, but it says nothing about Paul's own personal relationship to that empire. See further H. Rosin, "Civis Romanus sum," *NedTTs* 3 (1948–49)

123

16-27; H. J. Cadbury, *The Book of Acts in History* (London: Black, 1955) 58-85; E. Brewer, "Roman Citizenship and Its Bearing on the Book of Acts," *ResQ* 4 (1960) 205-19; A. N. Sherwin-White, *Roman Society and Roman Law in the New Testament* (Sarum Lectures 1960-1961; Oxford: Clarendon, 1969) 144-71; G. Kehnscherper, "Der Apostel Paulus als römischer Bürger," *SE II* (TU 87), 411-40; C. Burchard, *Der dreizehnte Zeuge: Traditions- und kompositionsgeschichtliche Untersuchungen zu Lukas' Darstellung der Frühzeit des Paulus* (FRLANT 103; Göttingen: Vandenhoeck & Ruprecht, 1970) 37-39.

4. E.g., Jerome, *In Ep. ad Philem.* 1 (PL 26. 640).

5. R. Abba writes, "When Saul of Tarsus enters upon his missionary vocation in the Gentile world, his name is appropriately changed from the Hebrew form, Saul, to the Roman, Paul (Acts 13:9)" ("Name," *IDB* 3. 506). But this is an oversimplified way of presenting the matter.

6. See M. Lambertz, "Zur Ausbreitung des Supernomen oder Signum im römischen Reiche," *Glotta* 4 (1913) 78-143.

7. Compare Joseph Barnabas Justus (Acts 1:23; cf. 4:36); Simeon Niger (Acts 13:1).

8. See H. Danby, *The Mishnah* (Oxford: Oxford University, 1933, repr., 1964) 446.

9. Yet, curiously enough, never in 1 Thessalonians, Philippians, or Philemon. There may be allusions to the Old Testament in these letters, but there are no explicit quotations of it.

10. See pp. 64-65 below.

11. See pp. 29-31 below.

12. See C. F. D. Moule, "Once More, Who Were the Hellenists?" *ExpTim* 70 (1958-59) 100-102.

13. See S. K. Stowers, *Diatribe and Paul's Letter to the Romans* (SBLDS 57; Chico, CA: Scholars, 1981), and the literature cited there.

14. See H. D. Betz, "The Literary Composition and Function of Paul's Letter to the Galatians," *NTS* 21 (1974-75) 353-79; *Galatians: A Commentary on Paul's Letter to the Churches in Galatia* (Hermeneia; Philadelphia, PA: Fortress, 1979) 14-25. For Romans, see J.-N. Aletti, *Comment Dieu est-il juste? Clefs pour interpréter l'épître aux Romains* (Paris: Editions du Seuil, 1991).

15. See Aristotle, *Politics* 5.2.7 (1302b.35-38); part of Stoic philosophy, Cicero, *Or. Philip.* 8.5.15; Seneca, *Ep. mor.* 95.52; Plutarch, *Coriolanus* 6.3-4; *Moralia* 426A.

16. See further pp. 64-79 below.

17. See further *PAHT* PT §67-80.

## Notes to Chapter 2

1. The rabbinic character of this expression is well known; see Str-B 1. 691–94. Josephus emphasizes that this was characteristic of the Pharisees "who passed on to the people regulations handed down by former generations," the "tradition of the fathers" (*paradosis tōn paterōn, Ant.* 13.10.6 §297). He contrasts this custom with that of the Sadducees.

2. Josephus agrees with this estimate of the Pharisees, when he records that they "are considered the most precise interpreters of legal matters" (*met' akribeias dokountes exēgeisthai ta nomima, J.W.* 2.8.14 §162).

3. *Theology of the New Testament* (2 vols.; London: SCM, 1952), 1. 187 (his italics).

4. Ibid. (again his italics). Bultmann went so far as to query "to what extent he [Paul] had already appropriated in his pre-Christian period theological ideas of this syncretism (those of the mystery religions and of Gnosticism) which come out in his Christian theology."

5. Ibid., 188 (his italics).

6. For an assessment of such traces, see H. Ridderbos, *Paul: An Outline of His Theology* (Grand Rapids, MI: Eerdmans, 1975) 22–29.

7. See J. Neusner, "The Use of the Later Rabbinic Evidence for the Study of First-Century Pharisaism," *Approaches to Ancient Judaism* (BJS 1; ed. W. S. Green; Missoula, MT: Scholars, 1978) 215–28. See further J. Neusner, *The Rabbinic Traditions about the Pharisees before 70* (3 vols.; Leiden: Brill, 1971); or in abridged form, *The Pharisees: Rabbinic Perspectives* (Hoboken, NJ: Ktav, 1973).

8. See further D. Lührmann, "Paul and the Pharisaic Tradition," *JSNT* 36 (1989) 75–94. Lührmann analyzes the *Psalms of Solomon* and finds in them an expression of pre-70 Palestinian Pharisaism. "So the *Psalms of Solomon* leave us with two questions, the question of christology and the question of the Law, both questions coming together in what for Paul is the contrast between the righteousness which is of the Law and that righteousness which is of God by faith" (p. 89). If Lührmann is right, then there is some evidence of pre-70 Palestinian Pharisaic tradition in Pauline writings.

9. Str-B 3. 160; cf. 4. 559.

10. G. Bertram (*TDNT* 2. 646) admits the same thing.

11. "Further Messianic References in Qumran Literature," *JBL* 75 (1956) 174–87, esp. 176–77 (Document II).

12. "A Qumran Scroll of Eschatological *Midrāšîm*," *JBL* 77 (1958) 350–54.

13. See also 4Q174 1–2 i 6–7 (J. M. Allegro, *Qumrân Cave 4: I (4Q158-4Q186)* [DJD 5; Oxford: Clarendon, 1968] 53).

14. "Notes en marge du volume V des 'Discoveries in the Judaean Desert of Jordan,'" *RevQ* 7 (1969–71) 163–276.

15. Ibid., 221.

16. See M. Burrows, *The Dead Sea Scrolls of St. Mark's Monastery* (2 vols.; New Haven, CT: American Schools of Oriental Research, 1950) 1. pl. 58; cf. pl. 60. Cf. J. Licht, *Megillat ha-Serakim: The Rule Scroll: A Scroll from the Wilderness of Judaea, 1QS 1QSa 1QSb: Text, Introduction and Commentary* (Jerusalem: Bialiq Institute, 1965) 135.

17. See M. Burrows, *The Dead Sea Scrolls of St. Mark's Monastery* (2 vols.; New Haven, CT: American Schools of Oriental Research, 1950) 1. pl. 58; cf. pl. 60.

18. See J. M. Allegro, *Qumrân Cave 4* (n. 13 above), 43–44.

19. See Y. Yadin, *The Temple Scroll* (3 vols. & supplement; Jerusalem: Israel Exploration Society, 1983), 2. 251.

20. Lit., "a summary of the deeds of the law." See E. Qimron and J. Strugnell, "An Unpublished Halakhic Letter from Qumran," *Biblical Archaeology Today: Proceedings of the International Congress on Biblical Archaeology, Jerusalem April 1984* (Jerusalem: Israel Exploration Society, 1985) 400–407, 429–31. The article appears in an abridged form with the same title in *Israel Museum Journal* 4 (1985) 9–12 (with a photo of one of the fragments, which contains a column and a half of eight lines of text, in which the phrase is found). The full text of 4QMMT can now be found in *QC* (1990), Appendix 2. The text as printed in *QC* is reproduced in R. H. Eisenman and J. M. Robinson (eds.), *A Facsimile Edition of the Dead Sea Scrolls, Prepared with an Introduction and Index* (2 vols.; Washington, DC: Biblical Archaeology Society, 1991) 1. xxxi.

J. T. Milik made reference to this text in *Les 'petites grottes' de Qumrân* (ed. M. Baillet et al.; DJD 3; Oxford: Clarendon, 1962) 221–25, referring to it as 4QMishn[ique]). Cf. Y. Yadin, *The Temple Scroll* (Jerusalem: Israel Exploration Society, 1983), 2. 213; J. M. Baumgarten, "The Pharisaic-Sadducean Controversies about Purity and the Qumran Texts," *JJS* 31 (1980) 157–70, esp. 163–64.

21. See F. M. Cross, "The Development of the Jewish Scripts," *The Bible and the Ancient Near East: Essays in Honor of William Foxwell Albright* (ed. G. E. Wright; Garden City, NY: Doubleday, 1961) 240, 186–88 (4QMMT is listed there as 4QS135[b]).

22. A. Sperber, *The Bible in Aramaic* (4 vols.; Leiden: Brill, 1959–1973) 1. 120. Tg. Neofiti reads: *wtzhr ythwn yt qyym' wyt gzyrt*

'*wryyt*' *wtwd*' *lhwn yt* '*rḥ*' *dy yhlkwn bh wyt ptgm*' *dy y*'*bdwn,* "you shall enlighten them about the covenant and the decision(s) of the law, and you shall make known to them the path by which they must walk, and the word that they shall do" (A. Díez Macho, *Neophyti 1* (6 vols.; Madrid/Barcelona: Consejo Superior de Investigaciones Científicas, 1968–79) 2. 119. For studies of the root '*śy* meaning "do" deeds prescribed by the law, see S. Liebermann, "Spr hm'sym – Spr hpsqym," *Tarbiz* 2 (1931) 377–79; S. Abramson, "Mlšwn ḥkmym," *Leš* 19 (1954) 61–71, esp. 61–65; D. Flusser, *Die rabbinischen Gleichnisse und der Gleichniserzähler Jesus* (Judaica et Christiana 4; Bern/Frankfurt am M./Las Vegas, NV: Peter Lang, 1981) 101–2; J. M. Baumgarten, *Studies in Qumran Law* (Leiden: Brill, 1977) 82–83; M. A. Friedman, "'m'śh gdwl': qt' ḥdš mn hm'śym lbny 'rṣ-yśr'l ('An Important Ma'ase' – A New Fragment of *Ma'asim livnei Eretz-Israel*)," *Tarbiz* 51 (1981–82) 193–205.

23. See the recent survey of the subject by T. R. Schreiner, "'Works of Law' in Paul," *NovT* 33 (1991) 217–44.

24. "The New Perspective on Paul," *BJRL* 65/2 (1982–83) 95–122, esp. 107 (his italics). See also his articles, "Works of the Law and the Curse of the Law (Galatians 3. 10–14)," *NTS* 31 (1985) 523–42; "Yet Once More – 'The Works of the Law': A Response," *JSNT* 46 (1992) 99–117.

25. "New Perspective," 110.

26. Ibid. Cf. C. E. B. Cranfield, "The Works of the Law' in the Epistle to the Romans," *JSNT* 43 (1991) 89–101.

27. "Works of Law as a Subjective Gentive," *SR* 13 (1984) 39–46. He builds his interpretation on a suggestion once made by E. Lohmeyer, who, however, did not exploit it in "Gesetzeswerke," *Probleme paulinischer Theologie* (Darmstadt: Wissenschaftliche Buchgesellschaft, 1954) 31–74; this appeared earlier in *ZNW* 28 (1929) 177–207.

28. Ibid. 45. Cf. H. Hübner, "Was heisst bei Paulus 'Werke des Gesetzes'? *Glaube und Eschatologie: Festschrift für Werner Georg Kümmel zum 80. Geburtstag* (ed. E. Grässer and O. Merk; Tübingen: Mohr [Siebeck], 1985) 123–33; T. R. Schreiner, "'Works of Law' in Paul," *NovT* 33 (1991) 217–44.

29. See further 1QH 1:21–23.

30. See further H. Ringgren, *The Faith of Qumran: Theology of the Dead Sea Scrolls* (Philadelphia, PA: Fortress, 1963) 63–67; F. Nötscher, *Zur theologischen Terminologie der Qumran-Texte* (BBB 10; Bonn: Hanstein, 1956) 183–85.

31. See further J. Reumann, *"Righteousness" in the New Testament: "Justification" in the United States Lutheran-Roman Catholic Dialogue.* With Responses by J. A. Fitzmyer and J. D. Quinn

(Philadelphia, PA: Fortress; New York LRamsey, NJ: Paulist, 1982) 31-32 (§62-63), 204 (§371).

32. Cf. Rom 9:15-18.

33. See Str-B, 1. 981-83.

34. "Perhaps the most important theological point differentiating the sectarians from the rest of Judaism was their belief in predestination, coupled with a dualistic view of the world (*praedestinatio duplex*)" (M. Broshi, *The Dead Sea Scrolls* (Tokyo: Kodansha, 1979) 15.

35. See further CD 2:7-13; 1QM 13:9-13. Also H. Ringgren, *The Faith* (see n. 30 above), 50-52; F. Nötscher, *Zur theologischen Terminologie* (n. 30 above), 173-74.

36. See A. Stewart, "Mystery," *A Dictionary of the Bible* (5 vols.; ed. J. Hastings; New York: Scribner, 1900-04) 3. 465-69, esp. 468. A. Loisy, *La naissance du Christianisme* (Paris: E. Nourry, 1933) 315-16. C. Guignebert, "Quelques remarques sur la perfection (*teleiōsis*) et ses voies dans le mystère paulinien," *RHPR* 8 (1928) 412-29. R. Kittel, *Die hellenistische Mysterienreligion und das Alte Testament* (Beiträge zur Wissenschaft vom Alten Testament ns 7; Stuttgart: Kohlhammer, 1924) 84-96.

37. Even before the Qumran Scrolls were discovered, this fact was realized; see D. Deden, "Le 'mystère' paulinien," *ETL* 13 (1936) 403-42. Cf. K. Prümm, "'Mysterion' von Paulus bis Origenes: Ein Bericht und ein Beitrag," *ZKT* 61 (1937) 391-425.

38. The best reading in 1 Cor 2:1 is *to mystērion tou theou,* (P[46], ℵ*, A, C), but some mss. (ℵ[2], B, D, F, G, Ψ, and the Koine text-tradition) read *martyrion,* "testimony," which is preferred by the *RSV*.

39. Note the interesting parallel to the Qumran use of *rāz* in *mystērion* of Eph 5:32, *to mystērion touto mega estin, egō de legō eis Christon kai eis tēn ekklēsian,* "This mystery is great, and I mean that it concerns Christ and the church." Here one finds the Greek preposition *eis* being used as Hebrew *'l* is used to express the reference, and the content of the mystery is the meaning of a biblical text (Gen 2:24), which has just been quoted. In this instance "mystery" is being used precisely as in 1QpHab 7:1-5. See further M. P. Horgan, *Pesharim: Qumran Interpretations of Biblical Books* (CBQMS 8; Washington, DC: Catholic Biblical Association, 1979) 237.

40. See further R. E. Brown, *The Semitic Background of the Term "Mystery" in the New Testament* (Facet Books, Biblical Series 21; Philadelphia, PA: Fortress, 1968) 22-30. Cf. J. Coppens, "'Mystery' in the Theology of Saint Paul and Its Parallels at Qumran," *Paul and the Dead Sea Scrolls* (ed. J. Murphy-O'Connor and J. H.

Charlesworth; New York: Crossroad, 1990) 132–58.

41. See LXX Deut 32:43; Gen 6:2; 1 Sam 14:52; 26:16; 2 Kgs 14:14; Ps 29:1; Wis 2:18. It reflects the Semitic use of Hebrew *ben* or Aramaic *bar* to designate a group of people.

42. This symbolic use is also found in Greek literature (e.g. Euripides, *Iphig. Taur.* 1026; Plutarch, *Moral.* 82B).

43. See Str-B, 2. 219: "überhaupt nicht nachweisbar."

44. See H. Braun, *Qumran und das Neue Testament* (2 vols.; Tübingen: Mohr [Siebeck], 1966), 1. 90–91.

45. The phrase also occurs in Luke 16:7; John 12:36 (cf. Eph 5:8, *tekna phōtos*). It may reflect an older Iranian background. Cf. P. J. Kobelski, *Melchizedek and Melchireša'* (CBQMS 10; Washington, DC: Catholic Biblical Association, 1981) 84–98.

46. See further J. A. Fitzmyer, "The Use of Explicit Old Testament Quotations in Qumran Literature and in the New Testament," *NTS* 7 (1960–61) 297–333; repr. with slight revision in *ESBNT*, 3–58.

47. See J. A. Fitzmyer, "Further Light on Melchizedek from Qumran Cave 11," *JBL* 86 (1967) 25–41, esp. 32–33; repr. *ESBNT*, 245–67, esp. 255–56.

48. "The Formulas Introducing Quotations of Scripture in the NT and the Mishnah," *JBL* 70 (1951) 297–307, esp. 298; repr., *Historical and Literary Studies: Pagan, Jewish, and Christian* (NTTS 8; Leiden: Brill, 1968) 52–63, esp. 54. The closest Mishnaic formula is *'āmĕrāh tôrāh*, "the law has said" (*Ḥullin* 12:5; cf. 1 Cor 14:34); or *hakkātûb 'ômēr*, "What is written says" (*Yebamoth* 4:4; cf. Rom 9:17; 10:11); or *kakkātûb bĕtôrat Môšeh 'abdĕkā*, "as it is written in the law of Moses your servant" (*Yoma* 3:8; 6:2; cf. 1 Cor 9:9).

49. See "The Use" (n. 46 above) 10–12. Cf. F. L. Horton, Jr., "Formulas of Introduction in the Qumran Literature," *RevQ* 7 (1969–71) 505–14.

50. *Paulus und seine Bibel* (Gütersloh: Bertelsmann, 1929) 43: "es fehlt jede Spur spätjüdischer Florilegien. Das bleibt zu beobachten."

51. Ibid., 52.

52. "Further Messianic References" (n. 11 above), 182–87 (Document IV). See also *Qumrân Cave 4:I* (n. 13 above), 57–60.

53. "The Period of the Biblical Texts from Khirbet Qumrân," *CBQ* 19 (1957) 435–40.

54. "Parallelomania," *JBL* 81 (1962) 1–13.

55. See R. Leivestad, "Hat die Qumranliteratur das Neue Testament beeinflusst?" *The New Testament Age: Essays in Honor of Bo Reicke* (2 vols.; ed. W. C. Weinreich; Macon, GA: Mercer University, 1984) 1. 259–70.

56. See *J.W.* 2.8,2–13 §119–61. Cf. G. Vermes and M. D.

Goodman (eds.), *The Essenes According to the Classical Sources* (Oxford Centre Textbooks 1; Sheffield, UK: JSOT Press, 1989) 34–57.
57. (SNTSMS 58; Cambridge, UK: University Press, 1988).
58. "An Unpublished Halakhic Letter," *Biblical Archaeology Today* (n. 20 above), 402.
59. *Israel Museum Journal* 4 (1985) 10–11.
60. "The New Halakhic Letter (4QMMT) and the Origins of the Dead Sea Sect," *BA* 53/2 (1990) 64–73, esp. 68–69. Cf. J. Baumgarten, "The Pharisaic-Sadducean Controversies" (n. 20 above).
61. L. H. Schiffman, "The New Halakhic Letter" (n. 60 above), 72 n. 15.
62. Of the Sadducees Josephus says, "They do away with fate entirely and remove God beyond, not merely the commission, but even the sight of evil. They say that human beings have free choice of good or evil, and that it rests with each one's will whether he follow the one or the other. As for the persistence of the soul after death, penalties in Hades, and rewards, they do away with them. . . . [T]hey are, even among themselves, boorish in their behavior, and in their intercourse with peers are as rude as with foreigners." (*J. W.* 2.8.14 §164–66).
63. "Some Remarks on the Qumran Law and the Identification of the Community," *Qumran Cave IV and MMT: Special Report* (ed. Z. J. Kapera; Krakow: Enigma Press, 1991) 115–17.
64. "The People of the Dead Sea Scrolls: Essenes or Sadducees?" *Bible Review* 7/2 (1991) 42–47.

## Notes to Chapter 3

1. See G. Ogg, *The Chronology of the Life of Paul* (London: Epworth, 1968); A. Suhl, *Paulus und seine Briefe: Ein Beitrag zur paulinischen Chronologie* (Gütersloh: Mohn, 1975); R. Jewett, *A Chronology of Paul's Life* (Philadelphia, PA: Fortress, 1979); J. Murphy-O'Connor, "Pauline Missions before the Jerusalem Conference," *RB* 89 (1982) 71–91; *St. Paul's Corinth: Texts and Archaeology* (Wilmington, DE: Glazier, 1983); G. Lüdemann, *Paul, Apostle to the Gentiles: Studies in Chronology* (Philadelphia, PA: Fortress, 1984); N. Hyldahl, *Die paulinischen Chronologie* (Acta theologica danica 19; Leiden: Brill, 1986); D. Slingerland, "Acts 18:1-17 and Luedemann's Pauline Chronology," *JBL* 109 (1990) 686–90.
These more recent studies depend in various degrees on earlier ones by D. W. Riddle, *Paul, Man of Conflict: A Modern Biographical Sketch* (Nashville, TN: Cokesbury, 1940) and J. Knox, *Chapters in*

*a Life of Paul* (New York: Abingdon-Cokesbury, 1950). See also Knox's earlier writings: "Fourteen Years Later: A Note on the Pauline Chronology," *JR* 16 (1936) 341–49; "The Pauline Chronology," *JBL* 58 (1939) 15–39.

2. *St. Paul's Corinth* (n. 1 above), 141.

3. *Chapters* (n. 1 above), 41–42.

4. *JBL* 74 (1955) 80–87.

5. The value of this article has been acknowledged by W. G. Kümmel in his *Introduction to the New Testament* (rev. ed.; Nashville: Abingdon, 1975) 254: ". . . Campbell has proved convincingly that the sequence of Paul's missionary activities that can be inferred from his letters is so remarkably compatible with the information from Acts that we have good grounds for deriving the relative chronology of Paul's activity from a critical combination of the information from Paul's letters with the account in Acts."

6. Cf. J. M. Gilchrist, "Paul and the Corinthians – The Sequence of Letters and Visits," *JSNT* 34 (1988) 47–69.

7. Paul uses *ta klimata tēs Achaias* in the same way in 2 Cor 11:10, and BAGD (436) explain it as "the province in its entirety." But in Rom 15:23, when Paul asserts that he has no longer any room (for work) *en tois klimasi toutois,* "in these regions," he is referring not to provinces, but to the area of the eastern Mediterranean where he has been evangelizing before he cast his gaze toward Rome and Spain in the west. Hence *klimata* (especially in the plural) could refer to areas greater than provinces.

8. For a different interpretation of these verses in Galatians 1 and 2, see M. J. Suggs, "Concerning the Date of Paul's Macedonian Ministry," *NovT* 4 (1960) 60–68, esp. 67.

9. For my attempt to work out the relative chronology of Paul's life and ministry, see *PAHT,* §P14–49, or *NJBC,* art. 79, §14–49.

10. See E. Bourguet, *De rebus delphicis imperatoriae aetatis capita duo* (Montpellier: C. Coulet & fils, 1905). Cf. A. Brassac, "Une inscription de Delphes et la chronologie de saint Paul," *RB* 10 (1913) 36–53, 207–17.

11. "Lettre de l'empereur Claude au gouverneur d'Achaïe (en 52)," *Les inscriptions du temple du IV siècle* (Fouilles de Delphes III/4; Paris: Editions de Boccard, 1970) §286. Cf. A. Plassart, "Inscription de Delphes mentionnant le proconsul Gallion," *REG* 80 (1967) 372–78; J. H. Oliver, "The Epistle of Claudius Which Mentions the Proconsul Junius Gallio," *Hesperia* 40 (1970) 239–40. See further J. Murphy-O'Connor, *St. Paul's Corinth* (n. 1 above), 141–52, 173–76.

12. The rest of the inscription is inconsequential. My translation follows the text as established by J. H. Oliver (n. 11 above); square brackets enclose restorations.

13. For the usual *cursus honorum* in such inscriptions, see M. P. Charlesworth, *Documents Illustrating the Reigns of Claudius & Nero* (Cambridge, UK: University Press, 1951) 11–14.

14. See G. Cousin et G. Deschamps, "Emplacement et ruines de la ville de KYC en Carie," *BCH* 11 (1887) 305–11, esp. 306–8. One should consult further *CIL* 6. 1256 and Frontinus, *De Aquis* 1.13. Cf. E. Groag, *Die römischen Reichsbeamten von Achaia bis auf Diokletian* (Akademie der Wissenschaften in Wien, Schriften der Balkankommission, Antiquarische Abteilung 9; Vienna/Leipzig: Hölder-Pichle-Tempsky, 1939; repr. Nendeln, Liechtenstein: Kraus, 1976) col. 3 §123; A. Brassac, "Une inscription" (n. 10 above), 44.

15. Dio Cassius, *Rom. Hist.* 57.14.5.

16. Ibid. 60.11.6; 60.17.3.

17. Among older writers who use the year 51–52, see A. Deissmann, *Paul: A Study in Social and Religious History* (2d ed.; New York: Doran, 1926) 272. E. Groag, *Die römischen Reichsbeamten* (n. 14 above), 32–35. J. Finegan, *Handbook of Biblical Chronology: Principles of Time-Reckoning* (Princeton, NJ: Princeton University, 1964) 317–18. These writers have also influenced more recent interpreters.

18. *Ep.* 104.1.

19. There is no reason to maintain with G. Lüdemann (*Paul* [n. 1 above], 163–64) that Claudius' letter was actually sent to Gallio's successor and that Gallio's term of office should be reckoned as falling chronologically "in the years 51/52 C.E." Cf. L. Hennequin, "Delphes (Inscription de)," *DBSup* 2. 355–73, esp. 367–68. J. Dupont, "Notes sur les Actes des Apôtres," *RB* 62 (1955) 45–59, esp. 55–56.

20. This is another item of Lucan data widely accepted by modern interpreters of Paul's missionary journeys: thus J. Murphy-O'Connor, *St. Paul's Corinth* (n. 1 above), 140; G. Lüdemann, *Paul* (n. 1 above), 178 (but cf. 158–59); R. Jewett, *A Chronology* (n. 1 above), 58, 91.

21. See n. 9 above.

## Notes to Chapter 4

1. The main articles of Jeremias that deal with the subject are the following: "Kennzeichen der ipsissima vox Iesu," *Synoptische Studien A. Wikenhauser zum siebzigsten Geburtstag . . . dargebracht . . .* (ed. J. Schmid and A. Vögtle; Munich: Zink, 1953) 86–93; "Abba,"

*TLZ* 79 (1954) 213–214; "Abba," *ZNW* 45 (1954) 131–32; "Abba," *Central Message of the New Testament* (London: SCM, 1965) 9–30; *Abba: Studien zur neutestamentlichen Theologie und Zeitgeschichte* (Göttingen: Vandenhoeck & Ruprecht, 1966) 15–67; *The Prayers of Jesus* (SBT 2/6; London: SCM, 1967) 11–65; *New Testament Theology: The Proclamation of Jesus* (New York: Scribner, 1971) 61–68. See further the bibliography of Jeremias's writings in E. Lohse et al. (eds.), *Der Ruf Gottes und die Antwort der Gemeinde: Exegetische Untersuchungen Joachim Jeremias zum 70. Geburtstag gewidmet von seinen Schülern* (Göttingen: Vandenhoeck & Ruprecht, 1970) 24–33.

It would be otiose to try to record the many exegetes and theologians who found Jeremias's interpretation convincing. Those who have been critical of it will be mentioned below at the proper occasion. The most significant contributions to the study of the problem since Jeremias's work have been E. Haenchen, *Der Weg Jesu: Eine Erklärung des Markus-Evangelium und der kanonischen Parallelen* (2d ed.; Berlin: de Gruyter, 1968) 492–494 n. 7a; and G. Schelbert, "Sprachgeschichtliches zu 'Abba,'" *Mélanges Dominique Barthélemy: Etudes bibliques offertes à l'occasion de son 60e anniversaire* (ed. P. Casetti et al.; OBO 38; Fribourg: Editions Universitaires; Göttingen: Vandenhoeck & Ruprecht, 1981) 395–447.

2. *Comm. in Matth.* 16.19; GCS 40. 541–42.

3. *Lib. interp. hebr. nom.*, De Marco, CCLat 72. 138. It is still queried in modern times whether Greek *abba* is "of Aramaic origin." See J. Barr, "Which Language Did Jesus Speak? – Some Remarks of a Semitist," *BJRL* 53 (1970) 9–29, esp. 16.

4. See J. Jeremias, *Prayers* (n. 1 above), 58; cf. M. Smith, *JAAR* 44 (1976) 726.

5. Three states of the noun are distinguished in Aramaic: *'ab,* "father" (absolute state: indefinite); *'ab,* "father of" (construct state [in this case, identical in form with the absolute], governing a dependent noun); and *'abbā',* "the father" (emphatic state: definite). *'Abbā'* as the emphatic state is the explanation used by G. Dalman, *The Words of Jesus* (Edinburgh: Clark, 1909) 192; Str-B 2. 49; G. Kittel, *TDNT* 1. 5 (but Kittel later changed his mind; see n. 7).

6. E. g. in Syriac: *'ābā'* (Peshitta of Luke 10:22). It is well known that words beginning with an *aleph* in Aramaic and vocalized with a short or reduced vowel often lost in time the whole first syllable by aphaeresis (e.g. *'ĕnāš,* eventually became *nāš;* the impv. *'ătā',* "come!" eventually became *tā'*); and the form *'ābā'* also became in some instances *bā'* (see *Tg. Onq.* of Num 3:24,30,35 [Hebrew *nĕśî' bêt 'āb* > *rab bêt bā'*]). In the Late phase of the language either the

consonant was secondarily doubled to form a closed syllable (as in *'abbā'*, perhaps under the influence also of *'immā'*) or the vowel of the first syllable was lengthened (as in *'ēnāš*, even fitted with *yodh* as a *mater lectionis*). See further my article, "Another View of the 'Son of Man' Debate," *JSNT* 4 (1979) 58–68.

7. See T. Nöldeke in the supplement to F. Schulthess, *Grammatik des christlich-palästinischen Aramäisch* (rev. E. Littmann; Tübingen, Mohr [Siebeck], 1924) 156; *Beiträge zur semitischen Sprachwissenschaft* (Strassburg: Trübner, 1904) 69–72; E. Littmann, "Anredeformen in erweiterter Bedeutung," *Nachrichten der königlichen Gesellschaft der Wissenschaften zu Göttingen, Phil.-histor. Kl.* 1916, 94–111; review, *Or* 21 (1952) 389; J. Barr, "Which Language" (n. 3 above) 16; J. Jeremias, *Prayers* (n. 1 above), 58; G. Schrenk, *TDNT* 5. 985 and n. 248; H. Conzelmann, *An Outline of the Theology of the New Testament* (New York: Harper & Row, 1969) 103 n. 3; G. Kittel, *Die Religionsgeschichte und das Urchristentum* (Gütersloh: Bertelsmann, 1932) 92–95, 146 n. 214.

Jeremias (*Prayers* [n. 1 above], 58), following T. Nöldeke, argues that "abba is a purely exclamatory form, which is not inflected and which takes no possessive suffixes." Though this is true, one has to ask when an emphatic state would ever undergo inflection or assume suffixes? That is simply not a valid argument. Moreover, the addition of an adverbial *-ā'* to *'ab* does not explain the doubled *b*.

Gustaf Dalman (*Grammatik des jüdisch-palästinischen Aramäisch* [2d ed.; Leipzig: Hinrichs, 1905] 90 (§7[e-f]) strangely tries to explain the final *-ā'* of *'abbā'* (which he says means "my father") as a shortened form of *-ay: ay > ê > ā*. But that anomalous explanation raises more problems than it solves.

8. See further Dan 2:29,31,37; 3:4,9,10,12,17,18,24; 4:19,21,24, etc. Cf. F. Rosenthal, *A Grammar of Biblical Aramaic* (Porta lingua orientalium 5; Wiesbaden: Harrassowitz, 1961) 43; H. Bauer and P. Leander, *Grammatik des Biblisch-Aramäischen* (Halle a. d. S.: Niemeyer, 1927) 92.

9. "Sprachgeschichtliches" (n. 1 above), 411.

10. Such a secondary doubling is found at times in other Aramaic words: *liššān*, "tongue" (from Protosemitic *lišānu*); *'attûn*, "oven" (from Protosemitic *'atūnu*); cf. C. Brockelmann, *Grundriss der vergleichenden Grammatik der semitischen Sprachen* (2 vols.; Hildesheim: Olms, 1966) 1. 69 (§41ff.).

11. J. Jeremias, "Abba," *Central Message* (n. 1 above), 18.

12. See further Sophocles, *Philoc.* 254; Plato, *Phae.* 227e ; cf. BDF §147; W. W. Goodwin and C. B. Gulick, *Greek Grammar* (Boston: Ginn and Co., 1930) §202, p. 1043; especially L. Radermacher,

*Neutestamentliche Grammatik* (2d ed.; HNT 1; Tübingen: Mohr [Siebeck], 1925) 52; G. B. Winer, *A Treatise on the Grammar of New Testament Greek* (Edinburgh: Clark, 1877) 227–28.

13. See J. H. Moulton, *A Grammar of New Testament Greek: Vol. I Prolegomena* (3d ed.; Edinburgh: Clark, 1978) 70.

14. The emphatic state could also be written as *'abbāh,* since the final *aleph* was often replaced by a final *he,* both consonants being vowel letters used to designate *ā.*

15. For an explanation of the various periods of Aramaic, see my article "Phases of the Aramaic Language," *WA,* 57–84.

16. See G. R. Driver, *Aramaic Documents of the Fifth Century* B.C. (Oxford: Clarendon, 1954) frg. 10:19 (neither the reading nor the interpretation is certain); *CIS* 2. 122:1.

17. See P. Dhorme, "Les tablettes babyloniennes de Neirab," *RA* 25 (1928) 53–82, esp. 60 n. 12 ([*N*]*ḥ br 'b'*); *CIS* 2. 122:2 (*'bsly br 'bh*); 154:1 (*šlm br 'b'*); *AP* 6:16 (*'ytn br 'bh*). This patronymic supplies the Aramaic background for the grecized name Barabbas in Mark 15:7.

18. See Hadad (*KAI* 216) 4,7,12; Bar Rakkab 3 (*KAI* 219) 4,5; Bar Rakkab 8 (*KAI* 217) 3; *Aḥiqar (AP* p. 213) 33; *AD* 3:2; 8:2,3; *BMAP* 4:19; Sefire II B 8; Sefire III 10,23,25.

19. Most of the following texts can readily be found in the collection published by D. J. Harrington and myself, *MPAT.* E.g. 11QtgJob 31:5 is *MPAT* 5, 31:5.

20. *MPAT* 29B, 2:19.

21. *MPAT* 20, 29.

22. *MPAT* 21, 2:12.

23. See J. T. Milik, *The Books of Enoch: Aramaic Fragments of Qumran Cave 4* (Oxford: Clarendon, 1976) 209.

24. *MPAT* 27, 11.

25. *MPAT* 19, 1:4; cf. J. T. Milik, *Books of Enoch* (n. 23 above), 300.

26. *MPAT* 64, 1:6,7; 3:1.

27. *MPAT* 29B, 2:24.

28. *MPAT* 95b.

29. *MPAT* 61, 1:3.

30. *MPAT* 145, c2. But it may mean simply, "The father buried his son," as I took it in *MPAT.*

31. *MPAT* 95a. See n. 33 below.

32. See P. Benoit et al., *Les Grottes de Murabbaʻat* (DJD 2; 2 vols.; Oxford: Clarendon, 1961) 1. 180.

33. *MPAT* 116. There is no certainty that *'b'* here is to be understood as the title; it could also be taken formally as "Father,

Yehoḥanan," especially if it were originally part of a family tomb. This presentation of the Palestinian material from Middle Aramaic was worked out independently of G. Schelbert ("Sprachgeschichtliches" [n. 1 above] 405–9), whose article came to my attention only after I had completed the research on the above data. But one will find a confirmation of my presentation in his work.

34. This is stressed as the origin of Mishnaic *'abbā'*, pace J. Barr ("Which Language" [n. 3 above], 16). As to whether the emphatic state makes good sense as a vocative and whether in Hebrew one uses a definitive article in saying "Father!" Barr should consult GKC §126e. That E. Haenchen (*Der Weg Jesu* [n. 1 above], 493) can deny that *'abbā'*, being Aramaic, is not found in the Mishnah, which is written in "pure Hebrew," is incredible. For its abundant use, he need only have consulted C. Y. Kasovsky, *Thesaurus Mishnae* (4 vols.; Jerusalem: Massadah, 1956–60) 1. 5.

35. See *m. Pe'a* 8:5; *m. Sabb.* 24:5; *m. Qidd.* 4:14; *m. Miqw.* 2:1; *m. Mid.* 2:6; *m. Maks.* 1:3; *m. Betsah* 3:8. For a list of rabbis who bore the title, see Str-B 1. 918–19.

36. See *m. Pe'a* 2:6. Here H. Danby (*The Mishnah* [Oxford: Oxford University, 1964] 12) strangely translates *'abbā'* as "his father," but notes that it may be "a proper name."

37. Ibid. 388. See further *m. Sanh.* 3:2 (*'b'* in parallelism with *'byk*, "your father"); *m. 'Ed.* 3:10; *m. Ketub.* 2:10; 12:3; *m. Ned.* 5:6; 11:4,11; *m. Git.* 7:6; 9:2.

38. See G. Dalman, *Grammatik,* 90 §14.7d. Danby (*The Mishnah* [n. 36 above]) so translates *'abbā'* in all the passages listed in n. 37, and in most of those listed n. 39.

39. See *m. Pe'a* 2:4; *m. Sabb.* 1:9; *m. 'Erub.* 6:2; *m. Ketub.* 13:5; *m. Ned.* 9:5; *m. Nazir* 4:7; *m. B. Bat.* 9:3 ("our father" [Danby]); *m. Sheb.* 7:7; 6:1; *m. Zeb.* 9:3; *m. Menah.* 13:9; *m. Tamid* 3:8; *m. Yad.* 3:1.

40. Under "classic targums . . . in the rabbinic period" I would normally include *Tg. Pseudo-Jonathan* (or *Yerušalmi I*), the *Fragmentary Targum* (or *Yerušalmi II*), and *Tg. Neofiti 1.* But I am limiting the discussion to the two that probably have the best claim to the earliest date among the "classic" targums. I use the latter term to distinguish them from the Qumran targums. I reckon with the Palestinian origin of both *Tg. Onqelos* and *Tg. Jonathan,* but am reluctant to include them as writings of Middle Aramaic. I can admit the distinction that E. Y. Kutscher ("Mittelhebräisch und Jüdisch-Aramäisch im neuen Köhler-Baumgartner," *Hebräische Wortforschung: Festschrift zum 80. Geburtstag von Walter Baumgartner* [Leiden: Brill, 1967] 158–175, esp. 169) makes, separating the language of these two targums from that of Galilean and Babylonian

Talmud Aramaic; but they are still only an earlier form of Late Aramaic. They have too many morphological forms and syntagmemes that are not found in Middle Aramaic. See further A. D. York, "The Dating of Targumic Literature," *JSJ* 5 (1974) 49–62; and the articles on the various targums in the *Encyclopedia Judaica* (Jerusalem: Keter, 1972).

41. See "The Phases" (n. 15 above), 62, 71–74. See further A. Vivian, "Dialetti giudaici dell'aramaico medio e tardo," *OrAnt* 15 (1976) 56–60.

42. G. Schelbert ("Sprachgeschichtliches" [n. 1 above], 415) has included Hebrew *'ābînû,* "our father," in his discussion. This form is often introduced into the discussion because of the formula in the Matthean "Our Father," *páter hēmōn ho en tois ouranois* (Matt 6:9), which is never found in pre-Christian Jewish writings but has its counterpart in later rabbinic texts (see Schelbert, "Sprachgeschichtliches," 421–24). But it is really a distracting formula for the restricted scope of the *abba*-problem being discussed. With such a formula Jesus is depicted teaching his disciples to pray, but it says little about his own relation to God. Moreover, as Schelbert has shown, in *Tg. Onqelos* and *Tg. Jonathan 'ābînû* is consistently rendered in Aramaic as *'ăbûnā',* save for two places in Isaiah, where the absolute state *'ab* is used instead: *kî 'attāh 'ābînû* (63:16) becomes *'ărê 'at hû' děrahmāk 'alēnā' saggî'în mē'ab 'al běnîn,* "for you are the one whose mercy toward us is more than (that of) a father toward (his) children"; or *wě'attāh Yhwh 'ābînû 'attāh* (64:7) becomes *ûkě'an Ywy děrahmāk 'alēnā' saggî'în mē'ab 'al běnîn,* "and now Yahweh, whose mercy toward us is more than (that of) a father toward (his) children. . . . "

43. That the emphatic state *'abbā'* should be used to translate the Hebrew absolute *'ab* (without the article) is noteworthy. Such a use of the emphatic in an indefinite sense is hardly to be found in Middle Aramaic; but it is characteristic of Late Aramaic, where the note of determination is on the wane and *'abbā'* can mean not only "the father," but also simply "(a) father."

44. Hebrew *'ab 'ehād* becomes *'abbā' 'ăhad,* a strange use, since numerals are usually used with the absolute state. But again, in Late Aramaic this indefinite use of the emphatic is not surprising.

45. In the last instance *'ābî wě'immî* becomes *'abbā' wě'immā'* on the lips of a child.

46. Most of the further development can be found conveniently gathered in J. Jeremias, *Prayers* (n. 1 above), 15–29; but one must scrutinize the dates of the material used there by him. See also P. Grelot, "Une mention inaperçue de 'Abba' dans le *Testament Araméen de Lévi," Semitica* 33 (1983) 101–8.

47. The address *páter,* again in a corporate or national sense, is found in 3 Macc 6:3,8; cf. 5:7; 7:6. But this writing is not certainly of Palestinian provenience. Similarly, *páter* in Wis 14:3; cf. 2:16 (of a righteous individual); 11:10. On the significance of this usage, I see no reason to depart from Jeremias's interpretation (*Prayers* [n. 1 above], 18–29). Cf. W. Marchel, *Abba Père: La prière du Christ et des chrétiens* (AnBib 19; Rome: Biblical Institute, 1963).

48. See Ms. Adler 3053, photo and text of which are found in J. Marcus, "A Fifth MS of Ben Sira," *JQR* 21 (1930–31) 223–240, esp. 238 and pl. Cf. J. Jeremias, *Central Message* (n. 1 above), 17; he argues for the dependence of the formula used there on Exod 15:2, which also "occurs elsewhere in Sirach."

As Schelbert ("Sprachgeschichtliches" [n. 1 above], 416) notes, there is no instance of *'abbā'* in any Qumran Hebrew text, which is significant in view of the Mishnaic usage discussed above.

49. Compare *Jub.* 1. 24–25, where "father" is used in an echo of 2 Sam 7:14, now applied to "the children of Israel." Cf. *Jub.* 1:28; 19:29. The use in *T. Judah* 24:2 and *T. Levi* 18:6 is problematic, not being of certain pre-Christian origin.

50. See E. Schuller, "4Q372 1: A Text about Joseph," *RevQ* 14 (1989–90) 349–76, esp. 362–63.

51. The vocative *'by* might seem to be found in Sir 51:1, which in the Hebrew reads: *'hllk 'lhy yš'y 'wdyk 'lhy 'by.* That might seem to mean, "I shall praise you, my God, my salvation; I shall thank you, my God, my Father." (This verse is not preserved in the Sirach text of 11QPs<sup>a</sup> or of the Masada fragments.) The Greek text of the LXX, however, reads: *exomologēsomai soi, kyrie basileu, kai ainesō se theon ton sōtēra mou,* "I shall acknowledge you, O Lord [and] King, I shall praise you as God my Savior." This form is followed by the Latin Vulgate: *Confiteor tibi Domine rex et collaudabo te Deum salvatorem meum;* cf. the *RSV,* "I will give thanks to thee, O Lord and King, and will praise thee as God my Savior." But the Syriac form has *'wd' lk mry' mlk' w'šbḥ šmk mry' bkl ywm,* "I shall acknowledge you, O Lord [and] King, and I shall praise your name, O Lord, every day." The *NAB* has translated the Hebrew text of Sir 51:1 thus: "I give thanks, O God of my father; I praise you, O God my savior!" (transposing the two parts of the verse). M. S. Segal (*Sēpher ben Sîrā' haššālēm* [Jerusalem: Bialik Institute, 1958] 352) vocalizes the Hebrew consonantal text thus: *'ăhallelēkā 'ĕlōhê yiš'î '[ôdē]kā 'ĕlōhê 'ābî,* which means, "I shall praise you, O God of my salvation; I shall thank you, O God of my father." This is almost certainly the correct understanding of the Hebrew text; but it thus eliminates the address of God as "my Father." Cf. A. Strotmann,

*"Mein Vater bist du!" (Sir 51,10): Zur Bedeutung der Vaterschaft Gottes in kanonischen und nichtkanonischen frühjüdischen Schriften* (Frankfurter theologische Studien 39; Frankfurt am M.: Knecht, 1991).

52. *Prayers* (n. 1 above), 59. Jeremias claims that these instances are pre-Christian because they are told of sages who are dated to 90 B.C. (see p. 58 n. 32). But they are not found in any pre-Christian texts!

53. *B. Ta'anit* 23a; see L. Goldschmidt, *Der babylonische Talmud* (9 vols.; Berlin: Calvary, 1897–1935) 3. 491; translation from I. Epstein (ed.), *The Babylonian Talmud* (35 vols.; London, Soncino, 1935–1952) 23. 117.

54. *B. Ta'anit* 23b; the crucial words are *še'ên makkîrîn bên 'abbā' dĕyāhêb mîṭrā' lĕ'abbā' dēlā' yāhêb mîṭrā'*. Cf. L. Goldschmidt, *Der babylonische Talmud* (n. 53 above), 3. 494; translation from the Soncino ed., 23. 120.

55. "Sprachgeschichtliches" (n. 1 above), 398–405. Schelbert shows that the first passage is clearly a late insertion into the Babylonian Talmud from a story found in *m. Ta'an.* 3:8 (see also *y. Ta'an.* 3:10). His verdict: "This passage is then to be excluded as an instance of the pre-Christian use of *'abbā'*" (p. 400). Schelbert further quotes J. Neusner to the effect that the second passage is "very late." For his verdict, see p. 405.

56. *Prayers* (n. 1 above), 15, referring to S. V. McCasland, "Abba, Father," *JBL* 72 (1953) 79–91. To which one could now add the claim of M. Smith in his review of J. D. G. Dunn, *Jesus and the Spirit, JAAR* 44 (1976) 726: "But abba — something between 'Daddy' and 'Hey, pop' — comes from *lower class Palestinian piety* [my italics]. Since we have almost no other evidence for such piety — the rabbis and Qumranites were learned cliques — Jesus' usage cannot safely be supposed unique." Undocumented claim! If there is no evidence, how does Smith know?

57. *Prayers* (n. 1 above), 16. Does the "new vocabulary" possibly depend on Christian usage?

58. Ibid. 29 (his italics). Cf. *Abba,* 33. A similar, less documented position was held earlier by G. Dalman, *The Words of Jesus* (n. 5 above), 190–93; cf. G. Kittel, *TDNT* 1. 6.

59. *Prayers* (n. 1 above), 57.

60. *The Titles of Jesus in Christology: Their History in Early Christianity* (London: Lutterworth, 1969) 307. Cf. B. M. F. Van Iersel, *"Der Sohn" in den synoptischen Jesusworten* (NovTSup 3; Leiden: Brill, 1961) 183; J. D. G. Dunn, *Jesus and the Spirit: A Study of the Religious and Charismatic Experience of Jesus and the First*

*Christians as Reflected in the New Testament* (London: SCM, 1975) 21–26; *Christology in the Making: A New Testament Inquiry into the Origins of the Doctrine of the Incarnation* (Philadelphia: Westminster, 1980) 22–33.

61. *The Theology of the New Testament according to Its Major Witnesses, Jesus-Paul-John* (Nashville, TN: Abingdon, 1973) 40.

62. *Jesus the Jew: A Historian's Reading of the Gospels* (London: Collins, 1973) 210.

63. Ibid. 211.

64. See P. Blackman, *Mishnayoth* (7 vols.; 2d ed.; New York: Judaica, 1964) 1. 52–53. Cf. Anon., *Mšnywt: Sdr zr'ym* (6 vols.; New York: Om Publishing Co., 1947) *ad loc.;* E. Levy, *Mišnāh Mēpōrešet: Masseket Berākôt* (Tel Aviv: Sinai, 1911) 40; H. L. Strack, *Berakhoth: Der Mišnatraktat "Lobsagungen"* (Leipzig: Hinrichs, 1915) 10: "[. . . .] auf Gott [māqôm] zu lenken; W. H. Low, *The Mishnah on Which the Palestinian Talmud Rests: From the Unique Manuscript Preserved in the University Library of Cambridge* (Cambridge, UK: University Press, 1883) 2a: *lmqwm; Mishnayot: Seder Zera'im* (Stettin: R. Grassman, 1862) 1. 11: *lmqwm;* G. Surenhusius, *Mischna sive totius Hebraeorum juris. . . . systema. . .* (6 vols.; Amsterdam: G. & I. Borst, 1698–1703) 1. 17: *lmqwm;* A. L. Williams, *Tractate Berakoth (Benedictions): Mishna and Tosephta* (London: SPCK, 1921) 35: "upon God" (n. 6: "God. Lit. the Place").

65. *The Mishnah* (n. 36 above), 5.

66. See W. Baumgartner et al., *Hebräisches und aramäisches Lexikon zum Alten Testament* (5 vols.; Leiden: Brill, 1967–) 593a. This designation for God is found elsewhere in later rabbinic literature: *Gen. Rabb.* 68:9; *b. Sanh.* 50a; *b. Ab. Zar.* 40b; *b. Nid.* 49b; *b. Ber.* 16b; *Pesiqta Rabbati* 21:10.

67. See O. Holtzmann, *Berakot (Gebete)* (Die Mischna I/1; Giessen: Töpelmann, 1912). Holtzmann compares the form *'ăbîhem* with *'ābînû* of the prayer *Šemōnēh 'Eśrēh* 6 and comments: "wenn mit *'ābînû* der Vater des Volkes gemeint sein kann," i.e. in a nationalist, corporate sense.

68. See L. Goldschmidt, *Der babylonische Talmud* (n. 53 above), 1. 112. When the Babylonian gemara comments on *m. Ber.* 5:1 in *b. Ber.* 32b, nothing is said about this form of the Mishnaic statement. See L. Goldschmidt, 1. 122.

69. See p. 54 above.

70. Vermes also cites the text of *b. Ta'anit* 23b about Ḥoni and the children, used above. After considering such material, he pens a surprising conclusion, which scarcely flows from his preceding discussion: "If the reasoning followed in these pages is correct, the

earliest use of *son of God* in relation to Jesus derives from his activities as a miracle-worker and exorcist, and *from his own consciousness of an immediate and intimate contact with the heavenly Father*" (*Jesus the Jew* [n. 62 above], 211; the last italics are mine).

71. *Der Weg Jesu* (n. 1 above), 493.

72. Ibid.

73. See below, pp. 58–60. It might be well to recall that Heb 5:7–8 alludes to the Gethsemane scene, and although it does not use *patēr*, it speaks of Christ praying "to him who was able to save him from death"; and this he does precisely as *huios*, "son" (v. 8; cf. v. 5). This allusion would be a testimony independent of the gospel tradition.

74. *Prayers* (n. 1 above), 29–65. See further W. Marchel, *Abba, Père* (n. 47 above), 181–211.

75. *Prayers* (n. 1 above), 30 (his italics).

76. Ibid. 35–38.

77. Cf. the parallel in Matt 16:27, "his father."

78. See p. 51 above.

79. This formula is almost exclusively Matthean (see 5:16,45,48; 6:1,14,26,32; 7:11,21; 10:32,33; 12:50; 15:13; 16:17; 18:10,14,19,35; 23:9); cf. Mark 11:25.

80. One could add Luke 23:24, if the text-critical problem could be solved.

81. For Stages I, II, III of the gospel tradition, see my book *A Christological Catechism: New Testament Answers: New Revised and Expanded Edition* (New York/Mahwah, NJ: Paulist, 1991) 24–26, 134–40, 155–58.

82. *Der Weg Jesu* (n. 1 above), 493.

83. He refers to Str-B 1. 394, who cites the saying of Rabbi Ṣadoq from *Seder Eliyyahu Rabbah* 28.149, which H. L. Strack and G. Stemberger (*Introduction to the Talmud and Midrash* [Edinburgh: Clark, 1991] 339) says, "M. D. Herr dates it to the tenth century"! See Jeremias's comments on H. Braun, *Prayers* (n. 1 above), 54.

84. Ibid. 53–54.

85. Ibid. 62.

86. See the comment of M. Smith in n. 56 above.

87. *Prayers* (n. 1 above), 62.

88. *Der Weg Jesu* (n. 1 above), 492. Cf. J. Barr, "'*Abba* Isn't Daddy," *JTS* 39 (1988) 28–47.

89. See *Gnosis: La connaissance religieuse dans les épîtres de saint Paul* (Bruges: Desclée de Brouwer, 1949) 58–62. Cfr. R. Bultmann, *The History of the Synoptic Tradition* (Oxford: Blackwell, 1968) 159–60.

90. For further discussion of this question, see my commentary,

*The Gospel according to Luke* (AB 28-28A; Garden City, NY: Doubleday, 1981, 1985) 867-68.

91. See further M. Hengel, *The Son of God: The Origin of Christology and the History of Jewish-Hellenistic Religion* (Philadelphia, PA: Fortress, 1976).

92. E. Norden, *Agnostos Theos* (Stuttgart: Teubner, 1913; repr. Darmstadt: Wissenschaftliche Buchgesellschaft, 1956) 303-8; A. von Harnack, *The Sayings of Jesus: The Second Source of St. Matthew and St. Luke* (New York: Putnam, 1908) 272-301; R. Bultmann, *The History* (n. 89 above), 160; E. Klostermann, *Das Matthäusevangelium* (HNT 4; Tübingen: Mohr [Siebeck], 1926) 102; J. M. Creed, *The Gospel according to St. Luke* (London: Macmillan, 1953) 149; W. G. Kümmel, *Promise and Fulfilment* (SBT 23; Naperville, IL: Allenson, 1957) 41-42; G. Bornkamm, *Jesus of Nazareth* (New York: Harper & Row, 1975) 226; C. K. Barrett, *Jesus and the Gospel Tradition* (Philadelphia, PA: Fortress, 1968) 26; M. J. Suggs, *Wisdom, Christology, and Law in Matthew's Gospel* (Cambridge, MA: Harvard University, 1970) 71-97.

93. G. Dalman, *The Words of Jesus* (n. 5 above), 193-94; J. Chapman, "Dr. Harnack on Luke X 22: No Man Knoweth the Son," *JTS* 10 (1908-9) 552-66; R. Otto, *The Kingdom of God and the Son of Man* (London: Lutterworth, 1943) 235-36; W. Manson, *Jesus the Messiah* (London: Hodder and Stoughton, 1956) 103-9; T. W. Manson, *The Sayings of Jesus* (Grand Rapids, MI: Eerdmans, 1957) 79 ("no good reason for doubting its authenticity"); J. Schmid, *Das Evangelium nach Matthäus* (RNT 1; 5th ed.; Regensburg: Pustet, 1965) 198-99; J. Schniewind, *Das Evangelium nach Matthäus* (NTD 1/2; Göttingen: Vandenhoeck & Ruprecht, 1967) 148-53; A. M. Hunter, "Crux criticorum — Matt. xi. 25-30 — A Reappraisal," *NTS* 8 (1961-62) 241-49; A. Feuillet, "Jésus et la sagesse divine d'après les évangiles synoptiques," *RB* 62 (1955) 161-96, esp. 169-96.

See further R. Feneberg, "Abba-Vater: Eine notwendige Besinnung," *Kirche und Israel* 3 (1988) 41-52; W. A. VanGemeren, *"Abbā'* in the Old Testament," *Journal of the Evangelical Theological Society* 31 (1988) 385-98.

## Notes to Chapter 5

1. The literature on this passage is abundant. Apart from the standard commentaries on 2 Corinthians, see the following more important discussions: J.-F. Collanges, *Enigme de la deuxième épître de Paul aux Corinthiens: Etude exégétique de 2 Cor. 2:14-7:4* (SNTSMS 18; Cambridge, UK: University Press, 1972) 42-143; J. Dupont, "Le

chrétien, miroir de la gloire divine, d'après II Cor., III, 18," *RB* 56 (1949) 392-411; J. Goettsberger, "Die Hülle des Moses nach Ex 34 und 2 Kor 3," *BZ* 16 (1922-24) 1-17; A. T. Hanson, "The Midrash in II Corinthians 3: A Reconsideration," *JSNT* 9 (1980) 2-28; C. J. A. Hickling, "The Sequence of Thought in II Corinthians, Chapter Three," *NTS* 21 (1974-75) 380-95; M. Hooker, "Beyond the Things That Are Written? St. Paul's Use of Scripture," *NTS* 27 (1980-81) 295-309; J. B. Nisius, "Zur Erklärung von 2 Kor 3,15 ff.," *ZKT* 40 (1916) 617-75; K. Prümm, "Der Abschnitt über die Doxa des Apostolats 2 Kor. 3, 1-4, 6 in der Deutung des hl. Chrysostomus: Eine Untersuchung zur Auslegungsgeschichte des paulinischen Pneumas," *Bib* 30 (1949) 161-96, 377-400; "Israels Kehr zum Geist: 2 Kor 3,17a im Verständnis der Erstleser," *ZKT* 72 (1950) 385-442; S. Schulz, "Die Decke des Moses: Untersuchungen zu einer vorpaulinischen Überlieferung in II Cor 3:7-18," *ZNW* 49 (1958) 1-30; H. Ulonska, "Die Doxa des Mose," *EvT* 26 (1966) 378-88; W. C. van Unnik, "'With Unveiled Face': An Exegesis of 2 Corinthians iii 12-18," *NovT* 6 (1963-64) 153-69; repr. *Sparsa collecta: The Collected Essays of W. C. van Unnik: Part One* (NovTSup 29; Leiden: Brill, 1973) 194-210.

Further literature can be found in the discussions of Paul's opponents in Corinth: C. K. Barrett, "Paul's Opponents in II Corinthians," *NTS* 17 (1970-71) 233-54; G. Bornkamm, "The History of the Origin of the So-Called Second Letter to the Corinthians," *NTS* 8 (1961-62) 258-64; G. Friedrich, "Die Gegner des Paulus im 2. Korintherbrief," *Abraham unser Vater: Juden und Christen im Gespräch über die Bibel: Festschrift für Otto Michel* (AGSU 5; ed. O. Betz et al.; Leiden: Brill, 1963) 181-215; D. Georgi, *Die Gegner des Paulus im 2. Korintherbrief: Studien zur religiösen Propaganda in der Spätantike* (WMANT 11; Neukirchen-Vluyn: Neukirchener-V., 1964) 258-82; J. J. Gunther, *St Paul's Opponents and Their Background: A Study of Apocalyptic and Jewish Sectarian Teachings* (NovTSup 35; Leiden: Brill, 1973); M. Rissi, *Studien zum zweiten Korintherbrief: Der alte Bund—Der Prediger—Der Tod* (ATANT 56; Zurich: Zwingli, 1969) 22-64.

2. See further "New Testament Kyrios and Maranatha and Their Aramaic Background," *TAG,* 218-35.

3. Perhaps one should also add 1 Cor 1:19-20; 2:16; 2 Cor 6:2.

4. See "Qumran and the Interpolated Paragraph in 2 Cor 6:14-7:1," *ESBNT,* 205-17.

5. See "A Feature of Qumran Angelology and the Angels of I Cor 11:10," ibid. 187-204; cf. J. Murphy-O'Connor, "Sex and Logic in 1 Corinthians 11:2-16," *CBQ* 42 (1980) 482-500.

6. See A. Deissmann, *Licht vom Osten* (4th ed.; Tübingen: Mohr

144       ACCORDING TO PAUL

[Siebeck], 1923) 12–13; cf. B. Powell, "Greek Inscriptions from Corinth," *AJA* 2/7 (1903) 26–71, esp. 60–61 (§40); H. N. Fowler (ed.), *Corinth* (16 vols.; Athens: American School of Classical Studies, 1929– ) 8/1, §111.

7. So S. Schulz, "Die Decke" (n. 1 above); D. Georgi, *Die Gegner* (n. 1 above), 274–82.

8. *Der zweite Korintherbrief* (MeyerK 6; 9th ed.; Göttingen: Vandenhoeck & Ruprecht, 1924) 112.

9. *An die Korinther I/II* (HNT 9; 5th ed. rev. by W. G. Kümmel; Tübingen: Mohr [Siebeck], 1969) 111.

10. See e.g. H. Ridderbos, *Paul: An Outline of His Theology* (Grand Rapids, MI: Eerdmans, 1975) 224–25.

11. It does recur in the hortatory passage of Rom 12:2; and in the deutero-Pauline letter, Eph 4:22–24.

12. The verb does occur in Symmachus' translation of Ps 33:1, but that is a different Greek translation of the Old Testament, one that dates from a later (Christian) period.

13. See further H. L. Strack and G. Stemberger, *Introduction to the Talmud and Midrash* (Edinburgh: Clark, 1991) 21.

14. See W. Baird, "Letters of Recommendation: A Study of II Cor 3:1-3," *JBL* 80 (1961) 166–72.

15. See further B. Cohen, "Note on Letter and Spirit in the New Testament," *HTR* 47 (1954) 197–203; B. Schneider, "The Meaning of St. Paul's Antithesis 'the Letter and the Spirit,'" *CBQ* 15 (1953) 163–207; H. Liese, "De spiritu et littera," *VD* 11 (1931) 225–29.

16. I.e. *a minori ad maius;* see H. L. Strack and G. Stemberger, *Introduction* (n. 13 above), 21.

17. See "Paul and the Law," *TAG,* 186–201.

18. We cannot enter here into the detailed exegesis of this assertion, which identifies "the Spirit" with "the Lord." For some recent literature on the problem, see M. Dibelius, "Der Herr und der Geist bei Paulus," *Botschaft und Geschichte: Gesammelte Aufsätze 2* (Tübingen: Mohr [Siebeck], 1956) 128–33; J. D. G. Dunn, "2 Corinthians iii. 17 – 'The Lord Is the Spirit,'" *JTS* 21 (1970) 309–20; A. Feuillet, "Le Seigneur qui est l'Esprit et le Christ, miroir et image de Dieu (2 Co. III, 17-18; cf. IV, 4-6)," *Le Christ, sagesse de Dieu d'après les épîtres pauliniennes* (EBib; Paris: Gabalda, 1966) 113–61; P. Galetto, "'Dominus autem Spiritus est,'" *RivB* 5 (1957) 254–81; A. Giglioli, "'Il Signore è lo Spirito,'" *RivB* 20 (1972) 263–76; D. Greenwood, "The Lord Is the Spirit: Some Considerations of 2 Cor 3:17," *CBQ* 34 (1972) 467–72; I. Hermann, *Kyrios und Pneuma: Studien zur Christologie der paulinischen Hauptbriefe* (SANT 2; Munich: Kösel, 1961) 38–56; E. Larsson, *Christus als Vorbild: Eine*

*Untersuchung zu den paulinischen Tauf- und Eikontexten* (ASNU 23; Uppsala: Almqvist & Wiksell, 1962) 275–93; S. Lyonnet, "S. Cyrille d'Alexandrie et 2 Cor 3,17," *Bib* 32 (1951) 25–31; C. F. D. Moule, "2 Cor 3.18[b] *kathaper apo kyriou pneumatos,*" *Neues Testament und Geschichte: Historisches Geschehen und Deutung im Neuen Testament: Oscar Cullmann zum 70. Geburtstag* (ed. K. Baltensweiler and B. Reicke; Zurich: Theologischer-V., Tübingen: Mohr [Siebeck], 1972) 231–37.

19. See J. Dupont, "Le chrétien" (n. 1 above); N. Hugedé, *La métaphore du miroir dans les épîtres de saint Paul aux Corinthiens* (Neuchâtel: Delachaux & Niestlé, 1957) 25–33, 64.

20. See further "'To Know Him and the Power of His Resurrection' (Phil 3:10)," *TAG,* 202–17.

21. See E. L. Sukenik, *The Dead Sea Scrolls of the Hebrew University* (Jerusalem: Magnes, 1955) pl. 38. Sukenik reads *l'w[rtw]m;* others prefer *l'w[rty]m,* a dual of fem. *'wrh,* "light of day."

22. A very fragmentary text (1QH 3:3) resembles the foregoing:

[          ]*lî ha'îrôtāh pānay*[          ].

[          ]You have illumined my face for me. . . (Ibid. pl. 37).

23. Ibid. pl. 38.

24. See D. Barthélemy and J. T. Milik, *Qumran Cave I* (DJD 1; Oxford: Clarendon, 1955) 126 (= 1Q28b).

25. M. Burrows, *The Dead Sea Scrolls of St. Mark's Monastery* 2/2 (New Haven: American Schools of Oriental Research, 1951) pl. 2. Cf. *1 Enoch* 38:4; R. Harris, "Enoch and 2 Corinthians," *ExpTim* 33 (1921–22) 423–34.

26. (SUNT 2; Göttingen: Vandenhoeck & Ruprecht, 1963).

27. See the discussion of "the Many" as a designation for "all the members" of the community by J. Jeremias, *TDNT,* 6. 538.

28. See 1QpHab 7:1–5 for an explanation of the source of the esoteric interpretation of the law given to the Teacher of Righteousness. Cf. CD 13:2; 14:6–8.

29. The motif of illumination is also found in a paraphrase of Deut 33:10a (MT "they will teach Jacob your ordinances, and Israel your law") used in 4QTestim 17–18: *wĕyā'îrû mišpāṭêkā lĕYaʻăqôb, tôrātĕkāh lĕYiśrā'ēl,* "they (the Levitical priests) shall make your ordinances shine for Jacob, your law for Israel" (see J. M. Allegro, *Qumrân Cave 4:I (4Q158-4Q186)* [DJD 5; Oxford: Clarendon, 1968] 58). Commenting on this text, T. H. Gaster related it to 1QH 4:6,23 and explained the illumination as "spiritual enlightenment," comparing Sir 45:17 (where to "enlighten" is parallel to "teach") and 2 Kgs 12:3; 17:28; Deut 17:11 (where Hebrew *yry,* "teach," is rendered by Greek *phōtizein,* "light up"). He found all this, as well as the New

Testament references to "enlightenment" (John 1:9; Eph 1:18; 3:9; Heb 6:4; 10:22; 2 Cor 4:4,6) to be influenced by contemporary Hellenistic exegesis derived from the mystery cults (see *VT* 8 [1958] 217-19, esp. 218-19). Cf., however, G. Vermes, *VT* 8 (1958) 436-38, for further references to the Old Testament (Prov 6:23; Isa 51:4; Hos 6:5; Zeph 3:5; Ps 43:2; 119:105) and less pertinent ones from later rabbinic literature.

30. See "'With Unveiled Face'" (n. 1 above), 195.

## Notes to Chapter 6

1. R. Scroggs, "Paul and the Eschatological Woman," *JAAR* 40 (1972) 283-303, esp. 297.

2. "A Feature of Qumran Angelology and the Angels of I Cor. xi. 10," *NTS* 4 (1957-58) 48-58; repr. with a postscript in J. Murphy-O'Connor and J. H. Charlesworth (eds.), *Paul and the Dead Sea Scrolls* (New York: Crossroad, 1990) 31-47; and in *ESBNT*, 187-204.

3. *Der erste Korintherbrief* (MeyerK 5; 9th ed.; Göttingen: Vandenhoeck & Ruprecht, 1910) 271.

4. "1 Corinthians 11:2-16 and Paul's Views Regarding Women," *JBL* 94 (1975) 94-110, esp. 101-8. See further "The Vocabulary of 11.3-16: Pauline or Non-Pauline?" *JSNT* 35 (1989) 75-88.

5. "On Attitudes toward Women in Paul and Paulist Literature: 1 Corinthians 11:3-16 and Its Context," *CBQ* 42 (1980) 196-215.

6. "1 Cor 11:2-16: One Step Further," *JBL* 97 (1978) 435-36.

7. "The Non-Pauline Character of 1 Corinthians 11:2-16?" *JBL* 96 (1976) 615-21; "Sex and Logic in 1 Corinthians 11:2-16," *CBQ* 42 (1980) 482-500; "Interpolations in 1 Corinthians," *CBQ* 48 (1986) 81-94. On the question of the unity and authorship of vv. 3-16, see A. C. Thiselton, "Realized Eschatology at Corinth," *NTS* 24 (1977-78) 510-26, esp. 520-21; J. P. Meier, "On the Veiling of Hermeneutics (1 Cor 11:2-16)," *CBQ* 40 (1978) 212-22.

8. "Paul and the Eschatological Woman" (n. 1 above) 298. Scroggs (n. 41) ascribes the meaning "source" to S. Bedale ("The Meaning of *kephalē in the Pauline Epistles,*" *JTS* ns 5 [1954] 211-15). Scroggs also attributes this meaning to H. Schlier (*TDNT* 3. 678), but Schlier's article does not use the word "source": "*Kephalē* implies one who stands over another in the sense of being the ground of his being."

9. "Paul and the Eschatological Woman" (n. 1 above) 298-99 n. 41.

10. "Paul and the Eschatological Woman: Revisited," *JAAR* 42 (1974) 532-37, esp. 534-35 n. 8.

11. Ibid.

12. "Sex and Logic" (n. 7 above) 491. He recalls that J. Weiss (*Der erste Korintherbrief* [n. 3 above], 269), H. Schlier (*TDNT* 3. 674) and H. Conzelmann (*1 Corinthians* [Hermeneia; Philadelphia, PA: Fortress, 1975] 183 n. 21) had already noted this earlier.

13. "Sex and Logic" (n. 7 above), 492.

14. In his commentary on 1 Corinthians in the *NJBC*, art. 49, §53, Murphy-O'Connor goes so far as to write: "Gk *kephalē* never connotes authority or superiority (*pace* S. Bedale, *JTS* 5 [1954] 211–15)." See further his article, "1 Corinthians 11:2-16 Once Again," *CBQ* 50 (1988) 265–74, esp. 269–70. Cf. J. Delobel, "1 Cor 11:2-16: Toward a Coherent Explanation," *L'Apôtre Paul: Personalité, style et conception du ministère* (BETL 73; ed. A. Vanhoye; Louvain: Leuven University/Peeters, 1986) 369–89.

Other commentators who have used "source" as the meaning of *kephalē* in 1 Cor 11:3 are C. K. Barrett, *A Commentary on the First Epistle to the Corinthians* (HNTC; New York: Harper & Row, 1968) 248; F. F. Bruce, *1 and 2 Corinthians* (NCBC; London: Marshal, Morgan & Scott, 1971) 103; D. Ellul, "'Sois belle et tais-toi!' Est-ce vraiment ce que Paul a dit? A propos de I Co 11,2-16," *Foi et vie* 88 (1989) 49–58.

15. See further S. Bedale, "The Meaning" (n. 8 above) 212.

16. See BDB 911. Cf. H. Wildberger, *Jesaja* (BKAT 10; 2d ed.; Neukirchen-Vluyn: Neukirchener-V., 1980) 264, 266, 282–84: "Haupt." Also O. Kaiser, *Der Prophet Jesaia: Kapitel 1-12* (ATD 17; Göttingen; Vandenhoeck & Ruprecht, 1970) 74.

17. This is the reading of ms. A; but ms. R uses *en archē tou laou,* which also appears in 20:9.

18. See further *De vita Mosis* 2.16 §82; 2.51 §290.

19. See further *De praem. et poenis* 20 §125: "For as in a living body the head is the first and best part and the tail the last and meanest . . . so too he means that the virtuous one (*ton spoudaion*), whether a single man or a people, will be the head of the human race (*kephalē . . . tou anthrōpeiou genous*) and all the others like parts of a body deriving their life from the powers in the head and at the top." In this instance, one may debate whether *kephalē* has the sense of "source."

20. The better reading here is *ho Christos* (found in mss. P⁴⁶, ℵ, A, Bᶜ, C, D², Ψ, and the Koine text-tradition). It creates a problem about which is the subject and which the predicate of the clause; but since *kephalē* is anarthrous in the two following clauses, and therefore to be taken as the predicate, I prefer to take *pantos andros hē kephalē* as the predicate in this clause too. The meaning of *ho Christos* is

also problematical and would call for a more developed discussion than is possible now.

J. Murphy-O'Connor (*JBL* 95 [1976] 617) maintains that it cannot be the risen Lord, but must be understood as the community of believers, as in 1 Cor 12:12. It might make some sense to say that Christ in that sense is the *kephalē* of every Christian, but it is baffling how Christ in that sense can be said to be *pantos andros hē kephalē*. The problem is still the same if one says that *ho Christos* is to be understood of the risen Lord. My own inclination is to think of the preexistent Christ. See further J. Weiss, *Der erste Korintherbrief* (n. 3 above), 270. Moreover, the collective sense of *ho Christos* seems out of place in the lineup of singulars, denoting individuals, *anēr*, *gynē*, and *theos*.

21. R. Renehan (*Greek Lexicographical Notes: A Critical Supplement to the Greek-English Lexicon of Liddell-Scott-Jones* [Hypomnemata 45; Göttingen: Vandenhoeck & Ruprecht, 1975] 120) has additional material for the metaphorical use of *kephalē*, but he does not mention this sub-category or give any of the evidence adduced in this chapter. The strange thing is that earlier editions of this lexicon did list such a metaphorical use of *kephalē*.

22. "The Meaning" (n. 8 above), 212.

23. After I had composed this study and submitted it to the editor of *NTS*, I learned through the kind cooperation of D. J. Harrington, editor of *NTA*, that the topic had been discussed by another New Testament interpreter. See W. Grudem, "Does *kephalē* ("Head") Mean "Source" or "Authority" in Greek Literature? A Survey of 2,336 Examples," *TrinJ* 6 (1985) 38–59. Grudem is in dialogue with other modern writers than those whom I have cited in the body of the chapter. Though both of us cite some of the same texts, some of my examples are in addition to those that he cites explicitly. He has, however, discovered many others that would supplement my list. Grudem supplies also a telling critique of the arguments of S. Bedale. But Grudem's discussion has also been criticized by R. S. Cervin, "Does *Kephalē* Mean "Source" or "Authority over" in Greek Literature? A Rebuttal," *TrinJ* 10 (1989) 85–112. See further W. Grudem, "The Meaning of *Kephalē* ("Head"): A Response to Recent Studies," *TrinJ* 11 (1990) 3–72.

See now my forthcoming article ("*Kephalē* in 1 Corinthians 11:3," *Interpretation* 47 [1993] 52–59) that salvages from these more recent studies what has to be said about the meaning of *kephalē* in this Corinthian passage. That article simply bolsters what is already presented here.

## Notes to Chapter 7

1. "Beiträge zur paulinischen Rhetorik," *Theologische Studien . . . Prof. D. Bernhard Weiss . . . dargebracht* (Göttingen: Vandenhoeck & Ruprecht, 1897) 165–247, esp. 190–91. See also his review of M. R. Vincent's commentary on Philippians (ICC), *TLZ* 24/9 (1899) 263.

2. A. Deissmann divided the passage into two strophes of seven lines each (*Paulus* [Tübingen: Mohr (Siebeck), 1911] 113; cf. *Paul: A Study in Social and Religious History* [London: Hodder & Stoughton, 1926] 193). H. Lietzmann was apparently the first to refer to the passage as a "christological hymn," which he set off not in strophes but only in seventeen lines of unequal length (*Mass and Lord's Supper* [fasc. 3; Leiden: Brill, 1954] 145). M. Dibelius also put it in rhythmic form (*An die Thessalonicher I, II; an die Philipper* [HNT 11; 3d ed.; Tübingen: Mohr (Siebeck), 1937] 74-78).

3. *Der Brief an die Philipper* (MeyerK 9/1; Göttingen: Vandenhoeck & Ruprecht, 1928; 14th ed., rev. by W. Schmauch, 1974) 90.

4. *Kyrios Jesus: Eine Untersuchung zu Phil. 2,5-11* (Sitzungsberichte der Heidelberger Akademie der Wissenschaften, Philosophisch-historische Klasse 1927–28/4; Heidelberg: Winter, 1928; 2d ed., 1961). Lohmeyer acknowledged the work of his forebears mentioned above in nn. 1–2. Cf. M. Black, "The Son of Man in Recent Research and Debate," *BJRL* 45 (1962–63) 305–18, esp. 314-15.

5. *Carmen Christi: Philippians ii.5-11 in Recent Interpretation and in the Setting of Early Christian Worship* (SNTSMS 4; Cambridge, UK: Cambridge University, 1967). Martin has a good survey of the literature on the passage and in particular notes (p. 30 n. 1) those who have followed the "six-strophe arrangement" of Lohmeyer. Martin's refinement of Lohmeyer's treatment reduces the hymn to six strophes of two lines each, after the omission of three glosses, "death upon a cross," "in heaven, on earth, and under the earth," and "to the glory of God the Father." Martin's book was reissued in 1983 (Grand Rapids, MI: Eerdmans) with a twenty-nine-page preface that evaluates selected recent studies; but there is no mention in that preface of the problems to which this paper addresses itself.

6. *Kyrios Jesus* (n. 4 above), 9.

7. Ibid.

8. Ibid. 5–6. (I have corrected the verse numbering.)

9. *Der Brief des Paulus an die Philipper* (THKNT 11; Leipzig: Deichert, 1935) 39–40.

10. "Kritische Analyse von Phil. 2,5-11," *Exegetische Versuche und Besinnungen* (2d ed.; 2 vols.; Göttingen: Vandenhoeck & Ruprecht, 1960, 1964) 1. 51-95, esp. 93; it originally appeared in *ZTK* 47 (1950) 313-60.

11. *A Commentary on the Epistle to the Philippians* (BNTC; London: Black, 1959) 76.

12. *New Testament Problems: Essays — Reviews — Interpretations* (New York: Macmillan, 1929) 141-50, esp. 148.

13. *Carmen Christi* (n. 5 above), 40-41. The Levertoff rendering has also been set in unpointed Hebrew type, but with a different spacing, by P. Grelot, "Deux notes critiques sur Philippiens 2,6-11," *Bib* 54 (1973) 169-86, esp. 176-77.

14. Ibid. 177.

15. See H. J. W. Drijvers, *Old Syriac (Edessian) Inscriptions* (SSS 3; Leiden: Brill, 1972).

16. It is wrong to speak of "the Palestinian targum" in the singular, since we have several targums from that area, and of diverse date, orthography, syntax, and wording. See further my article, "The Phases of the Aramaic Language," *WA,* 57-84, esp. 72-73.

17. Two lectionary forms of Phil 2:6-11 are preserved in Christian Palestinian Aramaic; see A. Smith Lewis, *A Palestinian Syriac Lectionary Containing Lessons from the Pentateuch, Job, Proverbs, Prophets, Acts, and Epistles* (Studia sinaitica 6; London: Clay and Sons, 1897) §10 (pp. 10-11), §75 (pp. 112-13). The problem is that no one can date these lectionary forms exactly or even approximately.

18. *MPAT* (1978). This manual appeared five years after Grelot's retroversion.

19. With most of the principles that Grelot has enunciated that should govern the retroversion ("Deux notes" [n. 13 above], 180-81) I am in agreement.

20. Ibid. 185. Grelot does not agree with the two-strophe, three-verse analysis of the hymn proposed by Lohmeyer. I shall comment on this below.

21. Grelot's transcription of the Aramaic text contains a few typographical errors, which I have permitted myself to correct; thus, *tômᵉmeh* and *šᵉmä* of v. 9 should read *rômᵉmeh* and *šᵉmâ; yésû'* of v. 10 should read *yésû'* (see v. 11); and *mᵉšîḥ* of v. 11 should read *mᵉšîḥâ*.

22. In the LXX the verb *hēgeisthai* renders a vast number of Hebrew or Aramaic verbs, one of which is *ḥāšab*.

23. See *Kyrios Jesus* (n. 4 above), 70-73.

24. See pp. 48-49 above.

25. *New Testament Problems* (see n. 12 above), 148.

26. See p. 91 above.

27. *Carmen Christi* (n. 5 above), 36.

28. This, of course, depends on the punctuation of that verse. For a discussion of the problems that the punctuation raises, see my commentary on Romans in *NJBC,* art. 51, §94, and a fuller treatment in the forthcoming full-scale commentary *Romans* (AB 33; Garden City, NY: Doubleday, 1993).

29. See further 1 Cor 1:13,17; 2:2,8; Gal 5:11,24; 6:12–14; Phil 3:18. The cross of Christ receives similar emphasis in the Deutero-Paulines too: Col 1:20; 2:14; Eph 2:16. By contrast, it is wholly lacking in the Pastorals.

30. See further U. B. Müller, "Der Christushymnus Phil 2,6–11," *ZNW* 79 (1988) 17–44.


# Notes to Chapter 8

1. See further my article, "Preaching in the Apostolic and Sub-apostolic Age," *Preaching in the Patristic Age: Studies in Honor of Walter J. Burghardt, S.J.* (ed. D. G. Hunter; New York/Mahwah, NJ: Paulist, 1989) 19–35. Cf. I. H. Marshall, "Preaching from the New Testament," *Scottish Bulletin of Evangelical Theology* 9 (1991) 104–17.

2. This situation arose not because of biblical scholars in the church, but because of liturgists who constructed the three-year cycle of readings. They should have had biblical consultants and made a better effort to coordinate the readings. The coordination is miserable in general.

3. "Caput et summa universae doctrinae christianae" (*Dispositio orationis in ep. ad Romanos: Philippi Melanthonis opera quae supersunt omnia* (ed. C. G. Bretschneider; 28 vols.; Halle: Schwetschke, 1934–60) 15. 445; cf. *Comm. in ep. Pauli ad Romanos (anno 1532),* ibid., 15. 495: "continet enim praecipuos proprios locos doctrinae christianae."

4. See pp. 12–16 above; cf. *PAHT* §PT67–80.

5. *Justification Today: Studies and Reports* (Lutheran World Supplement to No. 1, 1965; Geneva: Lutheran World Federation, 1965) I/1 (pp. 2–3): "The Reformation witness to justification by faith alone was the answer to the existential question: 'How do I find a gracious God?' Almost no one asks this question in the world in which we live today. But the question persists, 'How do I find meaning for my life?' When man seeks for meaning in his life he is impelled to justify his existence in his own eyes and before his fellow men.'"

6. See pp. 118–19 below.

7. See further J. W. Beaudean, Jr., *Paul's Theology of Preaching* (National Association of Baptist Professors of Religion Dissertation series 6; Macon, GA: Mercer University, 1988). J. Murphy-O'Connor, *Paul on Preaching* (New York: Sheed and Ward, 1963; updated in French form, *La prédication selon Saint Paul* [Cahiers de la Revue Biblique 4; Paris: Gabalda, 1966]).

# Biblical Index

153

# Index of Extrabiblical
# Ancient Writings

163

**Later Jewish Literature**

# Topical Index

168

# Index of Modern Authors